Corybantic Conversations
Imagined Encounters between Dalcroze, Kodály, Laban, Mason, Orff, Seashore, and Suzuki

Also by Edwin E. Gordon
Available from GIA Publications, Inc.

Advanced Measures of Music Audiation • G-3372M

Am I Musical: Discover Your Music Potential • G-6092K

Audie • G-3303M

The Aural/Visual Experience of Music Literacy • G-6384

Awakening Unborn, Newborn, and Young Children to Music
and the World of Audiation • G-7067

Clarity by Comparison and Relationship • G-7312

Designing Objective Research in Music Education • G-2976

Discovering Music from the Inside Out: An Autobiography • G-6762

Guiding Your Child's Music Development • G-3603K

Harmonic Improvisation for Adult Musicians • G-6650

Improvisation in the Music Classroom • G-6180

Intermediate Measures of Music Audiation • G-2593M

Introduction to Research and the Psychology of Music • G-4855

Iowa Tests of Music Literacy • G-3636M

Learning Sequences in Music:
A Contemporary Music Learning Theory • G-2345

Music Education Research: Taking a Panoptic Measure of Reality • G-6530

A Music Learning Theory for Newborn and Young Children • G-3487

Music Learning Theory: Resolutions and Beyond • G-6866

Musical Aptitude Profile • G-4304M

The Nature, Description, Measurement,
and Evaluation of Music Aptitudes • G-2996

Preparatory Audiation, Audiation, and Music Learning Theory • G-5726

Primary Measures of Music Audiation • G-2242M

Rating Scales and Their Uses for Measuring
and Evaluating Achievement in Music Performance • G-5856

Rhythm: Contrasting the Implications of Audiation and Notation • G-5511

Study Guide for Learning Sequences in Music:
A Contemporary Learning Theory • G-2345SG

Clarity by Comparison and Relationship:
A Bedtime Reader for Music Educators • G-7312

Whittled Wordscapes: Essays on Music and Life • G-7314

G-7394

Corybantic Conversations

Imagined Encounters between Dalcroze, Kodály, Laban, Mason, Orff, Seashore, and Suzuki

Edwin E. Gordon

Research Professor
University of South Carolina

GIA Publications, Inc.
Chicago

G-7394

GIA Publications, Inc.
7404 S. Mason Ave.
Chicago, IL 60638
www.giamusic.com

Copyright © 2008 GIA Publications, Inc.
All rights reserved.
Printed in the United States of America

ISBN: 978-1-57999-730-4

Contents

Preface vii

I:	Entrada and Introductions	1
II:	Purpose and Design	9
III:	Music Aptitude	13
IV:	Pedagogy	31
V:	Movement and Dance	49
VI:	Preparatory Audiation and Audiation	61
VII:	More Pedagogy	71
VIII:	Music Achievement and Grading	79
IX:	Tonal Essentials	91
X:	Rhythm Essentials	103
XI:	Instrumental Music	115
XII:	Patterns	127
XIII:	Improvisation	135
XIV:	Teaching, Learning, and Curriculum	145
XV:	Timbre/Range Preference	157
XVI:	Research	167
XVII:	Interlude	173
XVIII:	Neuroscience of Music	175
XIX:	Exire: Thanks and Farewell	183

Index 199

Preface

For some time, as I roam around in my psyche, I have projected imaginary conversations with illustrious music educators and others with tangential interests in music education who are no longer animate in earthly life. Based on their teaching, writings, and lectures, conjectures can be made about what might be the up-to-date nature of their overall thinking. Although many of their erstwhile thoughts are well documented, others, of course, are apocryphal, but nonetheless tantalizing. Much remains unknown. Even so, there are details about their personal lives and professional penchants that may be recaptured.

With apology for what could be considered a modicum of untoward transgression, though I hope not, what obviously and expressly clutches my curiosity pertains to the here and now. I wonder how these personages might actually interact in conversation about their bygone and possibly altered viewpoints concerning current music education in geographical areas they once inhabited and in which they commanded significant influence. What might they say to one another? I am compelled to create such a dialogue not only for my own satisfaction, but also because I am firmly convinced outcomes could be beneficial to music educators of all persuasions. Some of what we all believe we know "ain't necessarily so." There is, however, much of great value in what we do not know that undoubtedly could, if known, provide fruitful insight for evaluating our habitual pedagogical practices. After all, there are creators of the lore and carriers of the lore. The latter are bound to introduce desultory vicissitudes to the originator's thinking, if not outright infractions. Even after spending time engaging in broad reading in conjunction with taking copious notes to prepare for and accomplish this task I set for myself, I realize there is little doubt I remain a protean member of the group, specialists notwithstanding, of the unwittingly uninformed. Historical coverage and precision have not been all that good to us.

At this very moment, I am eighty years, two months, and a few hours old, or may I say young. At least my mind is amply agile to allow me to pursue this spellbinding endeavor. I have reason to believe it may prove to be one of the most valuable contributions to my colleagues and calling.

On the other hand, my seeming presumptuousness could agitate enough adversarial authorities so as to sully this document along with vitiating my erstwhile contributions. So be it. Time will tell.

For now, allow me to accept responsibility for errors of omission and commission that may be discovered. Conceivably of greater concern, however, is I was not able to invite additional departed persons who could have prolifically taken part in the discussions. Making ambivalent choices while adhering to practical limitations became an overwhelming, if not daunting, challenge. I turned to my notes as a guide to settle on inclusions, not to make exclusions. Circumstances permitting, and depending upon the reception of the forthcoming presentation, I am prepared to begin to write a sequel using a different playbill and a modified cast.

Bear with me and please remember, I do not pretend to be a historian. My approach was to use a personal lens as I focused on reasonable and engaging narrative, combining it with my interpretation of pedagogical theories and relevant related information. If you have suggestions and/or knowledge you believe might or should be included in a likely revision, it would be notably appreciated if you would pass them on to me along, if possible, with their sources. My email address is eegordon@gwm.sc.edu

I myself speak only through mouths of others, as an oblique, if not invisible, nonjudgmental catalyst to uncover issues and provide present-day information as needs arise. If, in fact, I could have been a real participant in the conversations with persons I hold in such high regard, my ever-present nonpareil dream would have come to pass. It is my hope your reading proves interesting and valuable. Above all, it would please me, even amid conceivable detected errata and misconceptions, if I have provoked you to join me in worthwhile stimulating thought.

I:
Entrada and Introductions

Greetings! My name is Corybant. I ask forgiveness for breaking your peaceful and silent pursuits. Perhaps I had no license to do so. However, I took advantage of a rare opportunity to separate you temporarily from nature's collective unconscious and bring us together. I discovered all of you are simultaneously inherent in the same sphere. I was hoping others could be included, but that seemed beyond the pale. I think I have done as well as I could to gather even seven of you. Please be patient. Shortly I will explain the purpose of my audacious plan. I have reason to believe you will be pleased with my initiative. It is nurtured by adamant curiosity.

Before I reveal my thoughts, I think it proper to introduce myself, and then I shall ask you to introduce, or reintroduce, yourselves to one another. I have made inquiries about whether any of you knew the others during your lives on earth. I obtained incomplete answers. Nonetheless, although not all of you might or could have had personal contacts, some recognized and were aware of the work of the others. Prior direct or indirect acquaintanceships, however, present no consequence for our mission.

I'm sure you don't know me, but maybe you know about me. I am a priest of the Phrygian goddess Cybele. Her rites are celebrated with music and ecstatic dancing. That should give you a clue about my predilection and why I issued this particular ensemble an invitation. As we engage in verbal exchange, your mutual interests will become evident. I can't imagine you are now any less caring, generous, and dedicated to your passionate endeavors than when you were experiencing earthly life.

The etymology of "ecstasy" harks back to the Greek *ekstasis*, currently carrying the meaning of intense joy and delight. Originally, it meant a trancelike condition marked by loss of orientation toward rational experience conjoined with concentration on a single emotion. Be that as it may, entertain no doubt: I anticipate our spoken interactions will be as enjoyable, informative, lucid, and cogent to all in the assemblage as well as the audience, that is, to those who, with your permission, will read a transcript of our dialogue taken by my shy, imperceptible aide. We don't, of course, have libations to offer, but I promise you will be delighted, if not enraptured, with what will prove to be inspiring conversation. I may be incorrect, but I have reason to believe, and hope, English will suffice as an appropriate language. Cybele has assured me, as a favor, those of you with need have been bestowed a rich vocabulary to listen to and speak the language with supererogatory comprehension. If you feel places provided for you are not comfortable, do not hesitate to move around.

In our presence are noted musicians, music educators, physical movement educators, dancers, and a psychologist, each of whom is a unique vessel of intelligence and knowledge. Of course, I know some of you have multiple interests and endowments. I attempted to locate the Swiss psychiatrist, Carl Gustav Jung, to ask him to join our mix as company to the sole psychologist, but I could not make contact with him. His human lifespan from 1875 to 1961 parallels most of yours, your aggregate being from 1792 to 1998, slightly more than 200 years, representing only a blip in celestial time. As a young man, Jung was a student of Sigmund Freud. Later in life Jung developed his own analytical supernatural theories that contrasted antithetically with—I might say they were even in diametrical opposition to—Freud's diagnostic insights. I am not sure about you, but as you might guess, my loyalty tilts toward the precociously imaginative younger man.

Be kind enough to introduce yourselves. With deference to age, we will begin with the oldest among you and progress chronologically. Once familiarity prevails and conversation begins, declaration of surnames rather than full names should preclude unnecessary formalities and unwieldiness for readers.

In accord with the scheme, we will begin with Dr. Lowell Mason.

I entered the earthly world in Medfield, Massachusetts, on January 8, 1792, and departed in Orange, New Jersey, on August 11, 1872. Being

I: Entrada and Introductions

a self-taught, eclectic musician, I specialized in composition of church anthems and hymns, conducting, organ performance, and publishing. Though I entered the business world as a paltry bank clerk in Savannah, Georgia, I ultimately became prosperous through the sale of collections of music I composed. An honorary doctorate was conferred upon me by New York University in 1835, one of the first instances of awarding that degree in the United States of America. I think you may know me best as an educator who adapted Johann Heinrich Pestalozzi's educational philosophy to teaching music in the Hawes Public Primary School in Boston, Massachusetts. I spent time in 1837 in Zurich, Switzerland, studying Pestalozzi's pedagogical methods. Though I traveled much, Boston ultimately became the center of my professional activities. In that regard, I might mention I, with George Webb, founded the Boston Academy of Music in 1832.

Please be next, Professor Émile Jaques-Dalcroze.

I'm amazed. Lowell was born almost three-quarters of a century before my birth in 1865. I say that because, even from the little I am aware of his accomplishments, I am convinced he was far ahead of his time. July 6th was my birth date, and Vienna, Austria, my birthplace. My parents, however, were French. Death came to me in Geneva, Switzerland, on July 6, 1950. After attending the gymnase and receiving a classical education in Belles-Lettres, I, Émile-Henri, studied composition seriously with Fuchs, Bruckner, Delibes, and Fauré, but I made my mark in teaching and administration. Swiss folk music will forever be my obsession. In collaboration with the French psychologist, Édouard Claparède, I created the system of Eurhythmics and founded the Institut Jaques-Dalcroze in Geneva. Genevans in the early 20th century, however, who lived according to rigid morality, were affronted by the corporal activities of students studying Eurhythmics. I made no attempt to ingratiate myself to them. Their greatest fear was some persons somewhere might be experiencing joy. Let me say, given the inevitability of triumph and dejection on earth, I am delighted to be here with élan, above it all, in your company. One more thing. I appropriated an additional name, Dalcroze, and appended it to my birth name, Jaques, so I would not be confused at the time with a composer of polkas in Bordeaux, France, who shared my appellation.

Now, Dean Carl Emil Seashore.

My name is Carl Emil Seashore, Sjöstrand in Swedish. Think of it. Émile and I lived virtually side by side in clock time. I was born a year later and died a year before. Thus, it should be no surprise I knew of his ideas indirectly through music educators with whom I was acquainted. My obituary recounts I was born in Morlunda, Sweden, on January 28, 1866. Our family moved to the United States of America when I was a child. Though not native-born, like Lowell, I was an American citizen when I died, on October 16, 1949, in Lewiston, Idaho. My wife, Mary Roberta Holmes, preceded me in death. Then I took up residence in the West with my youngest son, Sigfrid. I am the lone psychologist in the group. As an administrator and a professor, my interests are widespread, including an academic specialization in music aptitude under the broad umbrella of psychology of music.

Rudolf von Laban will now introduce himself.

You may not know of Pressburg, Pozony, where I was born. It was part of Hungary. Currently the name of the city is Bratislava, and the country is now called Slovakia. My birth and death dates were December 15, 1879, and July 1, 1958. I died in Weybridge, England. My parents were Hungarian, but my grandparents were English and French. Although educated as an architect at Ècoles des Beaux Arts in Paris, I became a professional dancer and choreographer. I gave years of thought to the anatomy of movement and movement education. Heidi Dzinkowska had great influence on my ultimate career choice. My system of dance notation, kinetography, was renamed Labanotation by the Dance Notation Bureau in New York City in 1953. In 1930, I was director of movement and choreography in the Prussian State Theatres in Berlin, and in 1934 I was director of the Deutsche Tanzbüne. In Addlestone, Surrey, England, I, with Lisa Ullmann in 1945, founded the Art of Movement School. Émile Jaques-Dalcroze and I had interests and students in common, for example, movement, dancing, theatre, and Isadora Duncan.

If I recall correctly, I, along with George Bernard Shaw and Darius Milhaud, were members of an audience in Hellerau, north of Dresden, Germany, who witnessed perhaps the final performance Émile produced, Gluck's Orfeo ed Euridice. The presentation combined music, theater, and dance. It was intriguing. I believe Émile knew of my work and I was respectful of his. We took different, though not highly dissimilar, paths to similar goals, each of us encountering heady disruptions beyond our control.

Alas, entanglements are a normal part of being human. In that regard, sadly, the German military insisted Émile was French, not Swiss. Therefore, he was forced to depart Germany at the onset of the Great War in 1914. Émile left a theatrical monument in Hellerau that represented so much of what he strived for throughout his professional career, never to go back. Ironically, the buildings remained dormant until Nazis and then Communists confiscated them to serve their deleterious, insidious needs.

May I present Dr. Zoltán Kodály.

Thank you. I am delighted. I, Zoltán Kodály, am humbled to be part of the meeting. Kecskemét, Hungary, was my birthplace. The event took place on December 16, 1882. My life ended in Budapest, Hungary, on March 6, 1967. My 85 years of earthly life were exciting. I enjoyed composing, which circuitously guided me into ethnomusicology and linguistics. With pride, and support from my esteemed colleague, Jenö Adám, I also addressed myself to Hungarian folk music and music education. In 1907, I was appointed professor in the Royal Academy of Music in Budapest, and in 1919, deputy director of the Budapest Academy of Music. It may surprise you to know I served as president of the Hungarian Academy of Sciences from 1946 to 1949. Béla Bartók's compositions, along with Claude Debussy's and Robert Schumann's, had enormous influence on my musical development. In 1913, Béla and I prepared a detailed paper titled, "A Project for a New Universal Collection of Folk Songs."

Lowell, I share your admiration for Johann Heinrich Pestalozzi's innovative pedagogical vision, which I embraced wholeheartedly and broadcast throughout Hungary. Émile, if I remember accurately, your mother was a piano teacher and taught in a Pestalozzian school. My belief was, and still remains, the future of a nation's music is determined in their schools. More poignantly, I insist a child's music education should begin at least nine months before the birth of the mother. I hope I am remembered for my contributions.

Next is Carl Orff.

Pluralism seemingly anathema to them, my work and the counterpoint of Zoltán Kodály's was, and still is, often discussed and interfaced, sometimes blended, even yoked, by music educators on earth, particularly in the United States of America. It is up to others to decide if, on the other hand, my compositions are on a par with Dr. Kodály's. I would be honored if that were generally acknowledged. In that regard, I might mention my most popular composition is a scenic cantata, *Carmina Burana*, but I am also known as an editor of Claudio Monteverdi's work. I hope it was meant as a tribute, not simply a diffident comment, when it was said I eschewed melody and counterpoint as well as exploited harmony and rhythm.

From 1915 to 1917, I conducted at the Munich Kammerspiele, and in 1918, I was a conductor at the Mannheim National and the Darmstadt Court Theatres. I completed music studies with Heinich Kaminski from 1920 to 1921. Whereas Zoltán had a passion for Hungarian folk music, mine was for German folk music, which I and Dorothee Günther, in Bavaria, Germany, incorporated into the philosophy of Elemental Music along with gymnastics, rhythm, and dance. Émile's Eurhythmics was an integral part of, and played a vital role in, our teaching.

As Corybant indicated, my name is Carl Orff. I made my entrance on earth in Munich, Germany, on July 10, 1895, and lifelessness came about in the same city on March 29, 1982. You, Corybant, if anyone, should know if there is any paranormal implication in my dying 100 years, to the year, after Zoltán was born. As I presume Zoltán did, I lived and worked in Europe throughout World War II.

Finally, Dr. Shinichi Suzuki.

Why I, Shinichi Suzuki, should have been invited to what I surmise is to become a music symposium is somewhat a mystery to me. I never envisioned myself a composer or great conductor, although I directed my own Tokyo String Orchestra. I don't even see myself as a superior performer. I enjoyed playing first violin, however, in a string quartet with my brothers. My fervor and obsession were dedicated to playing violin and string teaching. In 1930, I became president of the Teikoku Music School. In 1950, I organized the Kyoiku Kenkyu-kai in Matsumoto, Japan, where I taught instrumental music to students of all ages. I never wavered from believing that given proper instruction, all humans can enjoy as well as artistically perform great music, including, of course, the works of those in present company.

My unique and revolutionary philosophy of teaching students to play a music instrument, known and adopted throughout the world, is enshrined with my name. It is my conviction students should learn to play an instrument with musicality before applying themselves to learning how to read music notation. Teachers of the Suzuki method make a strict departure from traditional teaching. That is, students listening to and performing music before learning to read music notation is the direct opposite of the common practice of teaching students to read music notation before or concurrent with their acquisition of instrumental technique. Learning to listen to, speak, and read a language is the model for learning to listen to, perform, and read music notation. We read music notation, not music. Music should be in the mind.

If I calculate correctly, compared to my six colleagues, I was longest living on earth, almost 100 years, give or take a few months. My human history began in Nagoya, Japan, on October 18, 1898, and was fulfilled in Matsumoto, in the same country, on January 26, 1998. I am pleased to be included in the gathering.

II: Purpose and Design

I, Corybant, am amazed. Think of it. I understand the average longevity of humans in the Western world was 47 years at the beginning of the 20th century. Each of you defied that statistic by courageously dealing with earthly death, a natural consequence of earthly life, on your own inimitable terms. Congratulations! There must be something about being a sentient and sensitive artist in addition to a profound thinker that supports extended life. I use the word "thinker" rather than "intellectual" for good reason. In my view, intellectuals are those who generalize beyond their means. They would have no place here.

Now is an appropriate time to further explain why I drew you together. In a word, I am bored. For me, activity herein has been tranquil for too long. I am accustomed to ventures, both physical and intellectual. I need stimulation and incentive, not ennui. But for whatever recondite reason or reasons, Cybele is in a temporary slump that needlessly relegates me to soporific indolence, inertia if you will. Thus, I had to take matters into my own hands.

In my rummaging around, I became rapt with episodes that took place in the recent past and continue to take place on earth. I was looking for something different, if not more inspiring, to ponder than the same old humdrum I am typically embroiled in up here. Music education caught my fancy. There seems to be more than usual controversy in the profession, more so now than seemingly ever occurred in the past. I decided to confirm that and in doing so, I came upon many memorable and compassionate persons, such as yourselves.

As I said, the seven of you were all I could muster to request opinions about current developments below and how they may interact with concepts you entertained while on earth, and possibly with thoughts you may have embraced or are embracing in wraithlike contemplation. I do not expect you to declaim right from wrong. That is infantile behavior characteristic of earthlings who are bound by febrile egos, often aligned with criticism of those both living and deceased. I want thoughtful, congenial discussion, the type that avoids cross-purposes and parading of accomplishments. Fools' errands are the stuff human life is made of, and I am certain you are delighted to leave petards to the living. I trust you, as I, will become enthused and captured by the exchange of ideas. Let's hope my assumptions are accurate and there is no disappointment. Comity within civility is my wish.

I am compelled to utter a few more words before deliberations commence. You all appear to be content. I admire that, but I think I would be frustrated if I were to change circumstances with any of you. There is not one among you who did not pioneer and add distinctive and significant advancement to music education and general education. Yet, many of your contributions and insights go unnoticed and, perhaps more egregiously, are misunderstood by past and present humans. I believe those still living could benefit much if they would take time to learn of your comprehensive work rather than cut and paste sound bites in piecemeal fashion. They are uninformed to the extent of believing they have discovered imperative pedagogical directives. Ironically, most of your cohorts below would be astonished to learn there is actually no creativity. Flaunting solipsism and hubris, they simply and serendipitously rediscover eternal truths, some known and others unknown. There is essentially nothing new under the sun. Conceivably, when you were alive, you were guilty of the same errors of judgment, not always knowing you stood on shoulders of those who came before you, just as many of those below stand on yours. That, I think, is customary of those whom flesh adorns.

Being inexperienced with this type of modus operandi, I am not sure how to begin. I will risk asserting a topic I have in mind. Music aptitude, how does that suit you? Silence prevails! I hope you are not too polite to offer objections. I assume there is no disapproval.

Any one of you at any time may initiate or later enter the conversation. A personal request: Please keep in mind a remark of Thomas Jefferson's, third president of the United States: "There is no greater talent than not using two words when one will do." When he sarcastically queried, "How very is very," an embarrassed visitor quickly responded, "not very very." It is said the most stimulating conversation took place in the White House when Mr. Jefferson dined alone. Not a professional musician, he still possesses lofty wisdom and wide ranging interests. I wish I could have located him. I can't envisage how he might react to our conversation. Disarmed maybe, but definitely poetic. And, thinking about Thomas Jefferson's passion, I recall a statement made by George Bernard Shaw: "Please excuse me for writing a long letter. I didn't have time to write a short one."

My role, for the most part, will be to relax and enjoy the interchange. If necessary, and if not preempted, I, as an envoy, will impart ideas and information pertaining to what is currently taking place on earth. Let the tête-à-tête begin.

III: Music Aptitude

Seashore   Music aptitude you say. I take that as a cue to speak. That we all stand on shoulders of others, as you said Corybant, cannot be denied. The work of European and English researchers, such as Oswald Feis, T. H. Pear, Hans Rupp, and Carl Stumpf preceded mine. Their and others' curiosity and findings influenced my commitment to study the nature and measurement of musical talent. All undoubtedly were aware of Wilhelm Wundt's laboratory in Germany, dedicated to the new discipline of psychology. And, of course, Dr. Scripture, my professor at Yale, knew Wundtian psychology intimately. Round and round it goes.

Suzuki   Did I hear you use the term "musical talent?" I thought Corybant said "music aptitude."

Seashore   I was thinking in historical perspective. You see, shortly before and after the 1900s, we were not aware there was a difference between music aptitude and music achievement, if indeed different concepts of music aptitude and music achievement even entered our minds. Consciously or unconsciously, we described our investigations as the study of musical talent. "Talent," "gifted" and "musical," have come to be ambiguous words, unwittingly combining music aptitude and music achievement. My apologies. I aim to be precise. Music aptitude and music achievement will be distinguished from each other with care.

Suzuki   I appreciate that. However, I was hoping the word "talent" would be your expression of choice, and the word "aptitude" would be discarded. To my mind, there is no such thing as music aptitude, but I acknowledge the existence of music achievement. Music achievement is a result of environmental influences. I believe what you call music aptitude is really music achievement. Genetics? Nonsense.

Mason Shinicki, are you suggesting if our environmental influences were different from what they were, any one of us could have been a Johann Sebastian Bach or Wolfgang Amadeus Mozart?

Suzuki Yes, without uncertainty. To introduce another thought, ability breeds ability.

Seashore On what basis do you stake that claim?

Suzuki Common sense. Would Wolfgang have sustained such brilliance without the influence and authority of his father, Leopold, attention of his older, musically gifted sister, and the love of his mother? And think of Bach. He assiduously studied Vivaldi's scores and walked miles to hear Buxtehude perform. If I could have had one wish, it would have been to be a page turner for Bach. I might have become a great musician.

Mason Yes, but allow me to put the question another way. If you, Shinicki, or I had exactly the same formal structured and informal unstructured environmental opportunities as Mozart and Bach, do you believe we could have emulated those masters and attained comparable stature?

Suzuki I suppose that is an untenable question. How can we know? No two environments can ever be exactly the same. Perhaps nearly the same, but that's all.

Mason Your humanitarian ideas are admirable, Shinicki. Let me ask you another question. Do you suppose Zoltán Kodály and Carl Orff were born knowing how to compose? I think having potential to be a great composer is inborn; it is music aptitude, whereas learning how to compose is environmentally based, and that is music achievement. They are not the same. In fact, the former begets the latter. Do you disagree with that assumption, as did countless of Carl Seashore's critics when he was alive, and even now as he joins us here?

Frankly, at this point, I believe my thought processes are becoming disorganized.

Kodály I fear we are quibbling, and that is distressing Corybant, our gracious host. Let's hear more from Carl Seashore about music aptitude.

Seashore I'm convinced there is aptitude for science as there is aptitude for music. My bent is toward science, while you lean toward music. Being of Swedish Lutheran descent, I attended a country church regularly, heard music, and participated in singing. Yet my environment did not encourage me to study music. Even as a young boy, it was the phenomenon of inhibition and later, imagery, that seized my curiosity. When ravenous, I could actually smell eggs being fried for breakfast long before the stove was lit. But I don't believe I have aptitude for music.

Suzuki Are you saying one either has music aptitude or does not? Is it a dichotomy?

Seashore Yes. It was my belief one is either born with or without music aptitude. It is innate, hereditary if you will.

Mason That being the case, how can you contrarily report norms in the manual for the Seashore Measures of Musical Talent? If I understand correctly, norms suggest there are degrees of music aptitude, from low to high. Are you contradicting yourself, or am I missing the point?

By the way, I seem to remember in the 1919 version of your test battery, the word "talent" was used, but in the 1939 revision, it was changed to "talents." Was that modification of plural grammatical form obligatory?

Seashore The title was changed, but to explain now why would interdict our present topic. If you wish, we can plumb that depth later. In answer to your more stirring question, I must admit I did introduce confusion. I'm embarrassed to admit I surrendered to common practice. I used Alfred Binet's procedures for standardizing an intelligence test, including establishment of normative statistics, so it would be clear that my test was developed scientifically.

You know, scores on subtests in my battery cover a wide range of potentialities, and students who score below a certain point on a substantial portion of the subtests, necessarily including pitch and tonal memory, tend to be unsuccessful in the study of music.

Suzuki What is that score?

Seashore Somewhere below the lower two-thirds, certainly below average. I don't remember exactly.

Mason I gather you are suggesting there are levels of no music aptitude. Interesting! Isn't that tantamount to suggesting there are also levels of music aptitude?

Seashore Contradictory as that may ostensibly seem considering my previous assertions, there are degrees of music aptitude, but I don't think they are a result of inborn potential. I am uncertain about the nature of extra musical factors.

Suzuki Then I trust you agree environment does play a role in musical talent. Pardon me, but in spite of your explications, I feel more comfortable using the word "talent" rather than "aptitude."

Orff I'm curious about the alteration of the word "talent" to "talents." Please tell us about that Carl.

Seashore Allow me a short introduction before I answer. I took my undergraduate degree at Gustavus Adolphus College. After working my way through school by giving church sermons and clerking in stores, I graduated Yale with a Ph.D. in 1895, and became an assistant professor of philosophy at the University of Iowa. There was no

III: Music Aptitude

department of psychology at the time. Soon after arriving, I, assisted by graduate students, established a laboratory in 1897 and designed an audiometer, tonoscope, and chronograph in addition to other devices to initiate objective experiments in the psychology of music. I admired the work of William James at Harvard. In addition to music aptitude, I was interested in speech, audiometry, and euthenics, now called genetics. Among other ventures, I was instrumental in establishing a child welfare research station at the university.

It was patently obvious to me music aptitude is not a holistic capacity. It consists of various faculties, such as the senses of pitch, time, and consonance, as well as tonal memory and intensity discrimination. It was not long after publication of my test battery in 1919, however, objections were raised, particularly in England and Scandinavia, the United States notwithstanding. Challengers authored papers and created tests endorsing an interdependence theory of music aptitude, straightaway emphasizing elements of music aptitude are inseparable. They referred to their position as championing an omnibus theory in opposition to my mine, which was dubbed a specific theory. It was also common to hear the words "Gestalt" and "atomistic" used in that separation.

In response to adversity, I retitled the test battery by changing the word "talent" to "talents." I hoped that would indicate I had not changed my mind about music aptitude comprising multiple dimensions. To emphasize my belief, in neither version of the test battery did I offer norms for a total score.

Orff Do you still adhere to that position?

Seashore Without question. It is fact, not opinion.

Orff What makes you so sure?

Seashore Research of my own plus extensive contemporary research in the United States. The British and Europeans, however, still disagree.

Suzuki And I, as a Japanese, also disagree. In fact, I believe alleged music aptitude is a mirage regardless of its origin.

Seashore Shinicki, I neither mean to be gratuitous nor cosset you when I say believing or not believing in the concept of music aptitude seems to be akin to belonging to different religious denominations. I would like to persuade you to defer to the difference between subjectivity and objectivity, that is, if you are willing to recognize, not necessarily embrace, research findings.

Suzuki Go on, please. I like to think I am reasonable and clear sighted. Help me understand.

Seashore I must begin by explaining, while not petitioning for praise or professional compassion, I was a pioneer who broke new ground. I developed the first music aptitude test. I had nowhere to turn for advice other than my own predilections. Of course, I was knowledgeable of methods of standardizing a test, particularly in the realm of measuring intelligence, but the psychological constructs of music aptitude loomed large only in my own mind. How could I determine my assumptions were or were not credible? I, like any other scientist, had to engage in validity studies.

Suzuki Of course.

Seashore The validity studies, mostly conducted by graduate students, with my guidance, and professionals, some with whom I was not familiar, were fundamentally of two kinds. First, students' music aptitude test scores and their music achievement of various types were correlated. Second, investigations were designed to determine if practice, that is, taking the test more than once, and training, that is, pragmatically instructing students in understanding and responding to test questions comparable to those constituting the test, affected test results. In the latter case, if it could be shown test scores remained relatively stable after practice and training, it followed the test was not measuring music achievement but indeed, music aptitude.

In the former case, please remember correlation reveals relationship, not causation. We could not be sure whether high aptitude was the source of high achievement or the other way around. That is, we could not be confident previous exposure to music teaching was not responsible for superior scores on the music aptitude test. Overall, results were inconclusive, if not disappointing, due to contradictory data. That could be because either the subtests were bereft of validity or some researchers, primarily graduate students, were inexperienced and thus, studies were misappropriated and subject to misdirection.

Orff Tell us more about test validity. I know it is different from test reliability.

Seashore An exemplary long-term validity study was designed by Hazel Stanton and undertaken at the Eastman School of Music in Rochester, New York, in the first few decades of the twentieth century. My test was administered to undergraduates upon entrance to conservatory. Then data were collected as years passed to determine if music aptitude scores accurately forecast success in academic music in terms of graduation. Perhaps the study was ill-advised. Some low scoring students on the music aptitude test tended, without prompting, to discontinue attendance at conservatory. Thus, because of lack of wide variability in music aptitude scores, it was impossible to interpret resultant unwieldy correlation coefficients. No one, including me, was impressed with the results.

Orff What about reliability?

Seashore Reliability refers to the degree students' scores remain stable when the same test is administered under the same conditions on different occasions, the first administration usually occurring a week to ten days after the first.

I'm sorry for monopolizing the discussion, but a few more comments are obligatory. Since my time on earth, there have been advances in psychometric research. Briefly, a singular three-year longitudinal predictive validity study of a relatively new music aptitude test was conducted with elementary school students who had no previous formal music instruction. It was designed so students' continued participation was virtually assured. By correlating pre-instruction music aptitude scores with extensive post instruction music achievement data, it was concluded approximately 55% of the reason or reasons students achieve at various levels in school music may be attributed to their demonstrated music aptitude. Their achievement was caused by their music aptitude, not just related to it.

Orff Shinicki may care to continue this line of discussion, but I would like to alter the direction of the topic. I hope Zoltán might concur with my inquisitiveness.

Carl, as a corollary to pitch discrimination, do you truly believe one's ability to discriminate between two colors augurs artistic inclination? If so, who among us was not destined to be an outstanding painter?

Seashore I never implied that idea. What I said was if a student could not discriminate among different pitches, durations, and intensities, I doubted he or she could achieve musically.

Kodály So, your test has negative validity rather than positive validity. Is that why results of your validity studies, that is, data associated with your test battery, were uncertain?

Seashore Maybe so. I have left that to other researchers to investigate. But by the way, I steadfastly maintained in writing and speeches, for example at the National Music Supervisors' Association in St. Louis, Missouri, in 1919, that although students might excel in one type of discrimination on a given subtest, there was no guarantee they would distinguish themselves in one or more others.

Incidentally, which might be grist for the mill, I was asked to administer my test battery to music teachers in attendance at the conference. As would be expected, those who obtained abysmal scores denounced me along with the test. Some went so far as to accuse me of having personal ambition rather than professional motivation.

Mason Perhaps they were perturbed by your resolute persistence in the theory potential for music is hereditary. If that were confirmed, they probably wondered what was the point of universal demotic music education in the schools. Their teaching would be in vain, for naught. After all, if students could not learn, why teach them?

    Carl, I devoted a substantial portion of my life to convincing school administrators music should be a vital part of public school curriculums. I may have gone too far in my stentorian advocacy, but I believed including music as a viable subject in public education not only enhanced musical understanding, it also offered ancillary benefits related to discipline, health, and religiosity, while by no means discounting thinking for oneself.

Seashore Since I began my research, I continually have been admonished for being loose with the word "heredity." It is conceivable I should have used the word "innate" instead. At the time, heredity seemed to be indisputable. Largely because of Gregor Mendel's research with plants, we assumed musical competence, too, was predicated on ancestry. Current research on earth, if not holding heredity in abeyance, discounts that point of view. Shall I stand corrected for zealousness or hastiness?

    But in reference to your initial concern, Lowell, I did not advise that students who did not demonstrate high music aptitude should be neglected or denied an education in music. Nor did I suggest teaching them music would be a waste of time. To the contrary, I advocated music education as essential for all students regardless of their musical capacity. All of us are capable of listening to and enjoying music to some extent. That is not to say I recommended low scoring students on my test study a music instrument or engage in voice lessons in hopes of becoming professional musicians.

Kodály I agree with Carl Seashore. In my opinion, musicality is innate.

Orff Making the case in a more positive manner, I have no doubt musicality is inherent in all human beings.

Corybant All right, all right. I observe some restiveness. I, however, would still find continued interactions thought provoking. Thus, I petition we do not leave the subject of music aptitude prematurely. Let's pursue it somewhat more in terms of related facets. I trust my question will rouse your musical concerns.

Is what Carl labels music aptitude, call it whatever you wish—talent, ability, giftedness —relegated to simply discriminating variable elements heard in a sine wave? Is there no emotion in music? What about interpretation, expression, nuance, and creativity? Given my responsibilities to Cybele and my personal partiality, I am interested in these issues.

Jaques-Dalcroze I noticed Rudolf taking a deep breath in preparation to speak, but then he noticed my anticipation and graciously nodded to me to begin.

My silence until now must not be construed as disinterest. Far from it, I am enraptured with the wit and banter. I rarely had opportunity on earth to enjoy such repartee in serious trading of ideas. So, Corybant, I, for one, am not restless or disquieted.

Now, what about the essence of music, the libidinal role, paying homage to Freud and our host Corybant, of dynamics and tempo in ability to turn and appreciate musical phrases, and the like? Without those virtues coalescing with physical acuities, who cares anything otherwise about composition and measurement of music aptitude? Not me, for one.

Do you support me, Rudolf? I would think so, if I correctly remember a statement of yours a student passed on to me. In paraphrase, you said, one must experience all movement extremes to be a whole person. I ask, is not movement the basis of expression? Without expression, can sound be considered music? Can one react to music as a whole person? I doubt any learning can take place bereft of movement.

von Laban Émile. May we please postpone a discussion of movement until we overcome the present impasse? You and I have much to contrast about that vital subject. It is crucial movement not become a subsidiary inquiry.

Jaques-Dalcroze Of course. What now, Carl Seashore?

Seashore You are moving toward an examination of what are called preference measures. There is compelling germane history to impart. Again, I am sensitive about cornering the conversation. If that be the case, I offer my regrets, but should I disregard and not address your uncertainty, I would be remiss. At first blush it may seem what I put forward is parochial narrow-mindedness, but please be unwearied of me. Progress going on below is intellectually enticing.

Jaques-Dalcroze Proceed.

Seashore I realized early on I needed to address what you refer to as the emotional side of music aptitude. In the original version of my test battery, I included a test of the sense of consonance. Not going laboriously into all reasons for the misfortune, I will simply say the subtest repeatedly was shown to lack sufficient reliability, and thus that portended investigations of its validity would necessarily be futile.

The primary reason for this infirmity was the design of the test. It was a preference test. Unlike non-preference tests, there are no objectively correct answers to questions. Students were asked to indicate which part of a pair of sounds has more smoothness, purity, blending, and fusion. As I look back, I can imagine why students were inconsistent in their choices.

Ironically, in this connection I should report I coauthored the Meier-Seashore Artistic Judgment Test. Unfortunately, it did not fare any better than my musical judgment, that is, preference, subtest.

In the 1939 revision of the battery, I deleted the consonance test, substituted it with a non-preference timbre test, and added a test of rhythm. For the timbre test, students are to determine if two tones in a pair, which may or may not comprise different harmonic structure, sound the same or different.

Orff Admirable. True scientists redirect their efforts when objectivity points the way.

Seashore Herbert Wing, an English psychologist, took issue with the design of the test revision because it does not include any parts intended to measure musical expression. Toward the end of my professional career, he authored the Wing Standardized Tests of Musical Intelligence. It includes seven parts, four of which—rhythm accent, harmony, intensity, and phrasing—require preferential responses. A piano serves as the stimulus.

How were correct answers decided upon? Interestingly, snippets of well known extant music by established composers were performed by Wing's wife at the piano as intended, but also in what Herbert called mutilated fashion. The student has to say which rendition in the pair sounds better. Though created with good intentions, the test nevertheless is actually a music achievement test, not a music aptitude test, because, for all intents and purposes, it is a recognition test. Discounting his countrymen, most informed pundits agree that Wing was not any more successful than I.

Suzuki Does all this mean it is not possible to measure aptitude for musical expression and interpretation? If so, I think you have indirectly confirmed my position.

Seashore No, that is not so. Perhaps adding a coda to my summary may answer your question. Approximately ten years after my death, a young professor of music and education at the University of Iowa in Iowa City, my professional alma mater, became interested in the nature, development, measurement, and evaluation of music aptitude. He developed a music aptitude test battery that includes three preference subtests—phrasing, balance, and style. He conducted the three-year longitudinal predictive validity study I previously noted. In fact, that study was undertaken to investigate the fidelity of his test battery, the Musical Aptitude Profile. Students choose, from paired comparisons, which of two string instrument performances sounds better, not best, because both renditions of specially composed music in the pair have intentional faults.

How were these reliable tests validated? One way was that renowned musicians participated in an eight-year developmental program of the test battery by making choices. Unless nine of ten respondents preferred the same answer to a recorded test question, that query was either revised or removed from the relevant subtest. Given that history, I believe I can react positively to your concerns about the role of emotion in measuring music aptitude. I still believe, nonetheless, further improvements in testing musical preferences are in the offing, and will in time come to pass.

Suzuki Is there anything else of significance?

Seashore Yes. Contrary to my belief, contemporary researchers are convinced music aptitude is not dichotomous but rather, normally distributed. The range of music aptitude is from the 1st to the 99th percentile among typical groups of students. Approximately 1/6th have below average to low, 1/6th have above average to high, and 2/3rds have average music aptitude. Thus, the purpose of current tests is directed primarily to diagnosing and attending to individual musical differences and needs among all students.

   Moreover, of utmost importance, portions of longitudinal studies reveal disadvantaged students enrolled in impoverished schools display the same array of music aptitudes as do students from more affluent backgrounds. Although overall formal music achievement of the disadvantaged group is comparatively low, with proper instruction they achieve to the same degree as more socially fortunate students, and in some cases, even with superiority. Therein may lie one, if not the greatest, value of a music aptitude test battery: impartial identification of students with great promise that is not recognized by their parents or teachers.

Suzuki It seems plausible students might recognize great talent in themselves.

Corybant A comprehensive, though not conclusive, presentation. Émile and Shinicki, do you agree it is time to move on?

Mason If I am properly informed, there are some compelling final issues that may be of interest to the group. May we forestall closure for a few more moments?

Corybant What do you have in mind?

Mason Carl, are you aware of research addressing developmental and stabilized music aptitudes?

Seashore I am discomfited, Lowell, to answer that I am not. In the recent past I have been rapt with other events, so I am uninformed in that regard.

Mason The professor you have just spoken of is of the opinion there are two types of music aptitudes: developmental and stabilized. Your tests are designed for students nine years old and older. Inform me if I am wrong, but my guess is you found your tests unreliable when administered to younger students. Without going into great detail, this professor discovered that, when crafted differently for specific administration to children from three to eight years old, those in the developmental music aptitude stage, tests prove to be highly valid. In contrast to stabilized music aptitude tests you and he prepared for older students, he calls these developmental music aptitude tests.

Seashore What are the salient differences between the two types of tests?

Mason Fundamentally, with stabilized music aptitude tests, scores remain relatively stable upon repeated administration. That is not the case with developmental music aptitude tests, such as Audie, the Primary Measures of Music Audiation, and the Intermediate Measures of Music Audiation. Scores may fluctuate widely, even from month to month, depending on children's instruction in and exposure to music. Instability of scores, however, is not a function of unreliability of developmental music aptitude tests. When they are re-administered on adjacent days, or even twice on the same day, results are highly reliable.

Carl, with regard to your earlier statements about heredity and innateness, I know it will be rousing for you to learn current thought is music aptitude is a product of early environmental and innate factors. It is not solely one or the other. However, environmental influences, as explained, seem to have practically no effect on music aptitude scores of students nine years old and older, those students who have moved into the stabilized music aptitude stage.

Orff Lowell, Carl, what is audiation?

Mason A moment, please. It, like movement, deserves intense discussion. Later I will be happy to tell you what I have learned about it. For now, let me summarily say audiation is to music what thought is to language. Undoubtedly others will have additional information as well. I hope so.

Kodály I intuit we are about to leave the subject of music aptitude. That's all right with me, but, before that, I have two brief questions for Carl Seashore. Carl, if tests of stabilized music aptitude yield consistent scores upon repeated administrations, why do you report grade norms in your test manual that indicate scores increase with chronological age? In a way, this question, I guess, is related indirectly to ones raised earlier about normative degrees of music aptitude.

Seashore All tests of stabilized music aptitude have grade or age norms. Let me use the Musical Aptitude Profile and the Advanced Measures of Music Audiation as examples. It is true scores on stabilized music aptitude tests increase with advancing age. Remember, however, we are talking about raw scores. A raw score is the number of questions a student answers correctly. When it is said test results are stabilized, we are referring to standard scores, usually percentile ranks. Succinctly, although a student's raw score typically increases as he or she gets older, his or her percentile ranks remain relatively stable, usually within the range of one standard error of measurement. Don't feel alone, most persons unacquainted, and even some acquainted, with the interpretation of test results seem baffled by that noticeable anomaly in logic. But believe me, particularly in this case, reason supersedes logic.

Kodály My second question may be reminiscent of an earlier discussion. Free use of the word "discrimination" troubles me. I recall reading the manual for the Seashore Measures of Musical Talents and wondering why the option responses for some subtests are "same" or "different" but for the pitch test, they are "higher" or "lower." Does that not presuppose if students understand the musical meaning of high and low they demonstrate at least minimal music achievement? If am thinking straight, high and low are abstractions even when they are associated with music notation. That should further preclude the possibility that your test is one of music aptitude. Even if students were taught to perform without seeing music notation, but a teacher used the two words, the fact students were engaged in making music indicates they were not musical neophytes.

Seashore Goodness, I believe everyone should know the difference between high and low without having had music lessons.

Kodály You may be right in that assumption, but I am far from convinced. If I were to author a music aptitude test, I would be inclined to have all option responses be "same" or "different." In that way I would avoid the risk of unwittingly testing music achievement when my intent was to test what you call music aptitude. But, you are the authority.

Corybant If only Carl Jung were present. He could add a dimension to this ongoing discussion not yet voiced. I'm thinking specifically of something I recently read in the book, Musicophilia, written by Oliver Sacks, a professor of neurology and psychiatry at Columbia University in New York City. There is the prospect degeneration of the front parts of the brain, referred to as frontotemperal dementia, can spark a person into brio musicality who theretofore had little, if any, interest in listening to or performing music. Does that suggest the nature-nurture issue with regard to music aptitude is actually a non-issue?

Seashore I wish I could live my life over again! There are so many new challenging ideas that never crossed my mind when I was steeped in research. Thoughts of what I might investigate are exhilarating.

Corybant Carl, you can either change the person you were to the person you are or change the person you are to the person you were. It will not work both ways.

Seashore I choose, at least presently, not to make a choice.

Corybant The interactive gradations have been invigorating, so much so I need time to assimilate all I have heard. What say we disengage ourselves briefly and explore our surroundings? I see no disagreements, so let's disband. I assume one or more of you will have suggestions for further discussions. May I presume that is no longer solely my task?

IV: Pedagogy

Corybant I see five of us. Where are Zoltán and Carl Orff? I would not be taken aback to learn they are still engaged in conversation.

Carl, Zoltán, welcome. How about including us in your discussion?

Kodály Yes, both Carl and I would like to suggest the next topic.

Corybant Certainly.

Orff Zoltán and I have always shared an abiding interest in music pedagogy. We came from different directions, but were poised toward the same goal. Both of us attended to doing whatever we were able to foster a substantial music education for preschool children, school students, and adults. Although we shared the same product, our processes were different. You might say we nurtured contrasting pathways to attain similar purposes. There are music educators, however, who think our courses are contradictory, even shibboleths.

Though I cannot speak for Zoltán, I did not intend my teaching and lectures to spawn a specific method. I never had that in mind. My philosophy is an approach, not a method. As I often said, I planted the seeds and it was the teacher's responsibility to grow the garden.

Kodály Carl, may I interrupt? I understand why you choose to call the tradition you espoused an approach. Nonetheless, no matter what I might have suggested or proposed, my teaching has become more a method than an approach. Kodály teachers do more than follow a philosophy and create pedagogical material to support it. Specifically, elements and concepts are taught in sequence based on song idioms of immanent culture. Amid problem solving, the sequential paradigm is prepare, make conscious, reinforce, practice, and create.

Notice, I talk about the Kodály method. I did not actually write the curriculum, in fact I had little to do directly with that. A group of Hungarian music educators, including a formidable portion of dedicated musical nuns, who, using my vision, consulted with me and put the structure together. I was apprised periodically.

Orff Given your varied interests and obligations, I think it commendable you were able to stay in contact. But why weren't you more involved?

Mason Gentlemen. Carl's and Zoltán's proposal is enticing. I'm eager to hear what both have to say about their approach, system, or method, whichever is the preferred description, and how it was put into place. But first I must express a personal problem. I feel my professional life and work is being forsaken. Perhaps you knew the name Henry Mason, but most addressed me by my middle name, Lowell. Is that the reason when you talk of music education in the schools you tend to occlude me?

May I remind you that more than 100 years before either Carl or Zoltán became renowned in music education, at least in the United States of America, it was a result of my inexorable yeoman effort and determination in 1837 that music became an integral part of the public school curriculum in Boston, Massachusetts. I am not complaining or seeking accolades. I simply need recognition of the fact I made significant practical contributions, apart from historical implications, to consummating the ideal of music education for all, children and adults alike. I would like to be an integral part of the personal interchange. I sense you are overlooking me.

Kodály Our apologies.

Orff My sentiments, also. Further, it seems reasonable Lowell should begin the discussion. Some historical information about your omnibus accomplishments, Lowell, and early public school music education in

IV: Pedagogy

Boston would offer a smooth transition to the topic proposed. I have no reason to believe anyone would object to statements pertaining to your goals and bastion of achievements.

Mason Thank you. I'm uneasy because I feel I have forced myself upon you. I hope I don't bore you. I assure you, this is not a prosaic matter of personal vanity.

Corybant No need to be apprehensive. We are all friends.

Mason I am a music educator, first and foremost. True, I played organ and cello, and I composed and published hymns and anthems, but I don't pretend to be in Shinicki's class as a performer, nor do I fantasize being a composer of the caliber of Carl Orff and Zoltán, not to slight Émile. Your superiority in performance and composition is clear. But, when it comes to music education, and I bookend those two words with capitals "M" and "E," I declare myself peerless. Does that sound arrogant? I pray not. Most of my innovations have been diligently preserved. Even today they are common practice in many progressive music education curriculums. I am aware you all, in one capacity or another, are fabulous philosophers and teachers, and have gone beyond and improved upon my nascent initiatives.

Andrew Jackson served as seventh president of the United States of America from 1829 to 1837. He took advantage of increased presidential powers by proposing the model of universal education. The first public schools were opened in the 1820s. His proclamations encouraged me to pursue my dream of public school music education. I also had a hidden, though not enigmatic, agenda. The imperative I embraced was there would be a positive effect on church and university choirs if students learned music fundamentals in school at a young age.

Orff There is similarity here with what I call Elemental Music, which means belonging to the elements, near to earth. It is essential for spiritual growth and transcending the commonplace.

Mason Perchance I am making unwarranted assumptions about your knowledge of early music history in the United States of America. In the South and Midwest, several competing systems of shape-notes, also called buckwheat-notes and character notation, were in common use. The first system, introduced in 1801 by William Little and William Smith in The Easy Instructor, was based on "fasola" solmization. Each of four syllables, "fa sol la mi," had a different shape on the staff. Some editors simply inserted "F, S, L, M" on the staff rather than shape-notes. By the middle of the 19th century, seven shape-notes superseded use of only the original four. Rhythm was indicated in the convention manner, using stems, beams, and flags.

Orff Forgive me again, Lowell. By music fundamentals are you speaking of music theory and reading music notation.

Mason Yes.

Orff Well then, let's make it clear immediately that Zoltán and I held different views about music reading being a goal in teaching students. I never recommended solfege, reading, or music theory be taught to young students. Children become sensitive to sounds through non-intellectual incidental learning and movement like running, skipping, and jumping. Imitation first, then improvisation. All else later. Of course, music literacy is important and valuable, but it pales in comparison to students' development of a sense of self-confidence. The essence is simple: making and moving to music. Thus, I omitted music reading, or for that matter advanced music education, in my parameters.

Zoltán, if you don't mind, it would, of course, make more sense if you, rather than I, present your philosophy.

Kodály Contrary to Carl's position, I consider development of singing and music reading abilities to be of utmost importance. True, movement and rhythm games contribute to students feeling basic beats. Clapping and counting out rhymes, for example, develop a sense of meter, pulse, accent, and balance. However, I too, have what may be considered a pristine sequence that must not be precluded: singing,

IV: Pedagogy

reading, writing, ear training, improvisation, and listening. Teaching reading precedes engaging in improvisation. Although singing is the foundation for musical development, I endorse the principles of sound to sight, simple to complex, concrete to abstract, and the known to the unknown

Orff Interesting, I associate a different sequence with Kodály instruction.

Kodály What is it?

Orff Hearing, singing, showing, verbalizing, reading, writing, and creating.

Kodály Yes, many Kodály teachers express that sequence, and it does not impugn or obviate what I have said. Now, I believe Lowell has more to say.

Mason Thank you. After establishing a Sunday school for blacks, a music school for the blind, and a church in which I was in charge of music, serving as organist and choir director, I left Savannah and returned to Boston in 1827. Not surprisingly, as it was when I left, I found the musical abilities of adults and children to be deplorable. There was little tuneful singing in church choirs, understanding of rhythm was poor, keeping a steady beat was out of the question, and comprehending music notation was provincial, uncertain at best. I had to depend upon rote instruction to gain any semblance of musicality from those I shepherded. In 1830, by dint of determination, I even taught 150 to 200 students free of charge if they agreed to remain in class for at least one year. Also, need for qualified music teachers was abundant, so amid bitter political problems, I founded musical conventions to address the abyss. All seemed of no avail. Overall reform was an apparent necessity. Maybe I was being reproved for not following my parents' wish I not become a professional musician.

Hoping not to have been banal or galumph so far, I shall move to the essence of my story with concision. This should provide relevant background for our collective oncoming topic. My mission was to teach rudiments of music, music theory if you will, reading standard music notation, and singing. Though I engaged in class instruction, I was aware of individual musical differences among students, and I accepted the challenges of taking such variance into account.

Kodály Without, I hope, appearing unseemly, I must again suspend your presentation for a moment. Two phrases in your last remark startle me. The first pertains to reading standard music notation and second, to teaching to students' individual musical differences. Not to delay you interminably, I will direct my bewilderment to only the first, trusting we will have ample time later to discuss the second.

Lowell, you resided in the South long enough to become aware of the astonishing ability of people of Appalachia to sing in tune and read music notation using shape-notes. What prompted you to abandon the tradition of shape-notes? Further, why did you feel it necessary to teach rudiments of music in Boston? You had empirical evidence of the practical value of shape-notes, and it was clear theoretical knowledge was not a necessity for success.

Mason I have asked myself that many times throughout my professional zenith from 1827 to 1851. I will try to explain. Zoltán, my so-called conversion was precipitated by the work of Pestalozzi. I spent time with some of his followers, von Fellenberg, Pfeiffer, Nageli, and the great man himself, observing Pestalozzian innovative educational practices before the master passed in 1827. Adhering to step-by-step procedures emphasizing creativity, in conjunction with direct rather than vicarious experience, overwhelmed me. I was convinced the same philosophy applied to music—sound before sight, practice before theory, and singing before reading—could be followed with equally favorable effects in America. Not only would my constituency become respectable musicians, as an outcome, American culture would gradually move upward and become comparable to Western Europe. Candidly, I felt America was inferior in sophistication to countries across the ocean with which I had become familiar.

Elam Ives's prevailing book, published in 1830, was a watershed event. It prompted me to write a similar book, Manual for the Boston

Academy of Music, Instruction in the Elements of Vocal Music, on the System of Pestalozzi. It was published in 1834, and soon after, as I have mentioned, I collaborated in establishing the Boston Academy of Music in 1833. The academy was a satisfying outreach to Northeast and Southeast citizens who were interested in furthering their music education. I have been roundly criticized for, if not accused of, translating G. F. Kubler's text. It was published just before mine in Stuttgart, Germany. Perhaps some type of acknowledgement of his work might have been in order.

Orff Lowell, you reminded me of things I knew but others, I admit, evaded my purview. Now, however, let us please address ourselves to some tutorial details. With your permission, as continuation, I would like to restate what I professed heretofore and said during my time on earth. In all my work, my final concern is not with musical but rather, with spiritual expression. Remembering your statements, it would surprise me, Lowell, if you did not support, at least in part, my sentiments. Is that true?

Kodály Wait, Carl. You said we were to examine tutorial details. Not to denigrate your or anyone else's spiritual values, first things first.

Orff Would you like to begin, Zoltán?

Kodály Yes. Lowell, it is my understanding you visited John Curwen and were aware of Sarah Glover's work in England before I. Regardless, you, like I, were influenced by the English method of teaching reading of music notation. So much so, as you have said, you successfully convinced many of your Yankee countrymen to relinquish allegiance to shape-notes and use solfege in their teaching. I infer you brought back to America the movable "do" system, and if so, I would like to know your specific reasons for opposing, like I, the Continental system of immovable "do," or what some persons call fixed or Roman "do?" And, I seem to recall you were not terribly concerned with reading rhythm notation. Were you?

Mason Yes, the movable "do" system caught my fancy, and yes, I believed it represented more sophistication than shape-notes. Thus, it was a way to move American music education and appreciation to higher levels.

Kodály Did you adhere to John Curwen's initial use of a "do" based minor or Sarah Glover's intention of a "la" based minor?

Mason As a matter of fact, it was the idea knowledge of music theory and notation were unnecessary for one to distinguish between major and minor. That distinction could easily be accomplished through use of a "la" based minor. All a student had to do was associate "do" or "la" with the tonic, and that would reveal a piece of music to be in major or minor.

In the fixed "do" system used by Italians, French, Spanish, Portuguese, and others, C is always "do" whether music is major or minor. For them, solfege corresponds to letters in their respective alphabets. Regarding movable "do" with a "la" based minor, students need not contend with chromatic syllables, except "si" in harmonic minor. Of even greater importance, unlike the Continental system, the same syllable need not be used for different sounding pitches. Incompressible, at least to me, was students were, and still are being, instructed in that system to speak fixed "do" syllables, that is, they were not directed to simultaneously sing corresponding musical sounds. The purpose, I suppose, was essentially to increase speed in interpreting instrumental music notation.

Orff Lowell, why do use the word "tonic?" Does not a syllable relate to a resting tone, whereas a letter name indicates a tonic?

Mason As only an amateur historian, I do not feel qualified to answer that question.

Suzuki Am I correct in generalizing in the movable "do" system with a "la" based minor it would be logical to associate "re" with Dorian, "mi" with Phrygian, "fa" with Lydian, and "so" with Mixolydian?

Orff Yes, but you forgot Locrian, and it is associated with "ti." From what I discern, that complete spectrum is being used more and more in common practice in contemporary music education, even though no one knows for sure if and how those Greek dialectic words are associated with modern scales. Relationships represent a pastiche.

Jaques-Dalcroze OK. I've listened patiently so far, but wait a minute. Are you, Lowell and Zoltán, saying immovable "do" has no merit? If so, I guess I stand alone defending it, if for nothing else it is the nub of developing perfect pitch. No disrespect intended. I see no need to put the question to Rudolf and Carl Seashore, but what about you, Carl Orff and Shinicki? Did you ever use immovable "do?"

Suzuki I did. When studying violin with Karl Klinger in Berlin, Germany, I was introduced to Roman "do." No doubt it was of some value to me in facilitating my instrumental reading of standard music notation, but remember, I was capable of reading music notation before I arrived in Germany. I studied with Ko Ando in Tokyo before working with Herr Klinger. Seven years in all, from 1921 to 1928. I'm not sure how valuable it might have been if I had been a novice. It occurs to me, however, one must be familiar with music theory and music notation to fruitfully use fixed "do."

By the way, Èmile, do you have evidence immovable "do" teaches absolute pitch? If indeed you do, is it the best method of accomplishing what you consider to be an attribute? Isn't the source of so-called perfect pitch, in reality, genetic?

Jaques-Dalcroze Which question first?

Suzuki Èmile, before you answer, may I say something? Without posing as an expert, it is my humble opinion use of movable "do" would have more practical value than Roman "do" with youngsters, especially those with little or no knowledge of music theory and notation. My students sang but did not use any solfege. They listened, listened, and listened some more before they read music notation. The transition was smooth and natural, as it should be. It is no different from learning to read a language. How can one learn to read a language without having had adequate experiences in hearing it? So it is with the language of music. I'm not sure solfege of any type would have improved my students' achievement in music reading. More listening, undoubtedly, would have.

Carl Orff, what is your opinion?

Orff Music does not stand alone. It is bound by speech, movement, and dance. That is what I call Elemental Music. I did not, could not, and do not care an iota about solfege.

Kodály As I recall, Carl Orff said the Latin word *elementarius* means belonging to the elements.

Orff Yes, it does. Children's tonal understanding comes from surrounding folk traditions, and language forms the foundation for their rhythm dexterity. Why trouble and indoctrinate young ones with solfege? Go directly to the source. Need we intellectualize the obvious and natural? In praise of Pestalozzi, no pretense is necessary. I rest my case.

Kodály Among other attributes, solfege leads to aural memorization of intervals.

Jaques-Dalcroze I found solfege combined with rhythm and movement, both non-locomotor and locomotor, enhances overall understanding of music.

Orff Are you referring to fixed "do?"

Jaques-Dalcroze Yes. It may appear divergent from the belief not immediately combining tonal and rhythm elements is beneficial, but what I have said is a fact.

Kodály Èmile feels isolated in his belief and I do in mine. Calling what is done in my name in music education, an approach, a system, or a method, is immaterial. I would not deny adherents in Hungary have

IV: Pedagogy

created a method. What is the etymology of the word "method?" It means a path. Yes, students educated coincidentally with Kodály principles—there, I like that word "principles"—are taught solfege. And even more to the disdain of some among us, I also encouraged, and still do, use of rhythm solfege.

von Laban What is rhythm solfege? Are you referring to Labanotation?

Kodály No. You may not be aware of the work of the siblings Aime and Nanine Paris. They, along with Èmile-Joseph Chevé, Nanine's husband, carried forth in France Pierre Galin's attempt to remedy difficulties students encountered when being taught to read rhythm notation by counting and using time value names? In spite of Hector Berlioz' assistance, French authorities denounced the new idea of rhythm solfege as frivolous.

How it happened I am not sure, but John Curwen became informed of the newly developed French system and he Anglicized the syllables. When Curwen discovered the syllables were not well suited to English translation, he resorted to the use of dots, dashes, lines, and whatever, above and aside pitches on the staff to give meaning to intended rhythm. In my opinion, that was not much help. In fact, it created undue confusion. It was then, in addition to my concurrence with the value of teaching rhythm solfege, it became obvious to me stick notation would be a beneficial counterpart of tonal solfege.

Orff May we temporarily put aside rhythm solfege, stick notation, and yes, I know Èmile, you have not forgotten perfect pitch, and get back on track to the broader topic of overall pedagogy? No pun intended, we are not in harmony. Details can come later.

Kodály Move ahead, Carl, but we must return sooner or later to the role of this vital concept of the use of solfege in music education.

Orff I am not too proud to believe Dorothee Guenther in 1962 explained the essence, the ethos, if you will, of my philosophy better than I ever could have. I will paraphrase her. Children should accompany their rhythms, as they dance, with their own musical possibilities. To provide child-appropriate activities, so desperately needed for spiritual growth, original indivisibility for all humans in the elementary sense was once a fact of life. It should again be the goal in children's dance and music-making.

With that, Dorethee summed up my viewpoint. It does not imply a method. It offers self confidence to teachers to discover unique pedagogical implications, to understand music and movement are preeminently equal and interdependent. I have always been more interested in the practical than philosophical. I think John Dewey would have welcomed me into the company of pragmatists.

von Laban Method, approach, system, framework, model, principles, or whatever. What's the difference? Followers will do as they choose no matter what the creator had in mind. Do you actually think contemporary musicians perform Bach and Mozart as those composers intended? At best, composers of the past might today only vaguely recognize their own music. Yes, of course, instrumentation has evolved, but artistic interpretation vacillates, even in one's own musical development. In the latter regard, consider Glenn Gould's various interpretations of J. S. Bach's Goldberg Variations. So, I request, please let us reinstate our discussion of rhythm solfege and stick notation.

Jaques-Dalcroze Wait a moment. We forgot about immovable "do" and perfect pitch. Let's go in order.

Do I have scientific evidence immovable "do" begets perfect pitch? No! But my teaching experience indicates it does.

Kodály Some skeptical contemporary music psychologists claim perfect pitch is not so perfect, that it is unstable not only from day-to-day but from moment-to-moment. But let us say Èmile is correct. So what? Does it matter if one can name a pitch heard or produce it without a reference pitch? Because I am capable of both with a reasonable degree of accuracy, I am in a position, as I suppose Èmile and others are too, to express a discordant opinion without being discredited due to envy.

IV: Pedagogy

Yes, perfect pitch is advantageous if one is a conductor who typically reads untransposed scores, but equally disadvantageous to one who plays a transposing instrument. Sometimes persons with an acute sense of pitch cannot adjust to imperfections usually encountered in ensemble playing or when an accompaniment is supplied on a keyboard instrument typically tuned in equal temperament.

Moreover, how in the world does perfect pitch relate to musical expression? It doesn't. Which is more important, perfect pitch or musical sensitivity? Great artists may possess both, but if I were forced to make a choice, I would elect sensitivity. Èmile, as alluded to, would you say because I can distinguish among colors, that is, I have perfect color, the corollary to perfect pitch, that I have potential to be or I am an elegant artist? Are there not more compelling concepts to dwell on than purported perfect pitch in the music education of adults and children?

von Laban Still thinking about rhythm solfege and stick notation, I am inclined to believe explaining them might impinge on our understanding of movement and dance.

Kodály When I returned to Hungary from England, I was totally committed to providing appropriate music education for young children. The Hungarian system needed reform. Béla Bartók, Geza Revesz, a music psychologist and music educator, and I journeyed to Transylvania for a specific purpose. We believed the best way to recapture Hungarian culture from gradual erosion by German culture was to teach authentic Hungarian folk songs in primary schools.

Since there was a paucity of such music to be resurrected in Hungary, we traveled to Transylvania where indigenous folk songs, almost exclusively anhemitonic pentatonic and in duple meter, were still being performed. We recorded and brought them back to Hungary to be taught in schools. They formed the crux of future Kodály instruction, the core of which is based on the belief the path from music illiteracy to musical culture is through reading and writing music notation. That is not to say singing is unimportant. Sequentially, singing, being the most accessible instrument, a mainstay, provides the foundation for reading and writing music notation.

Mason I recently read what a Kodály biographer, Làszlò Eösze, wrote. I recall a poignant statement related to what Zoltán has just said. The following, though not a precise quotation, represents a reasonable rephrase. A thorough knowledge of material must precede everything, for everything else must be built only upon this knowledge. Any effort to achieve aesthetic results, which either precedes or discards this knowledge, is equivalent to building castles in Spain.

Seashore What does anhemitonic mean?

Orff A scale lacking semitones.

von Laban What about your connection to rhythm solfege and stick notation.

Kodály Yes, and I will also discuss the use of hand signs. First, rhythm solfege. You know about Chevé's syllables and Curwen's attempt to adapt them from French to English. Realizing the complexity of that system, I innovated a simpler one. Rather than signs, syllables are used for reading rhythm. Just as tonal syllables are called tonal solfege, rhythm syllables are called rhythm solfege. For example, two quarter notes in 2/4 are "ta ta," and two eighth notes, "ti ti."

von Laban What about triple meter?

Kodály That came later. Individual teachers created their own syllables. My immediate concern was meter of native Hungarian folk music, which is primarily duple. As with the tonal counterpart, anhemitonic pentatonic was crucial for the same reason. Major, minor, and other modes came later.

Mason Zoltán. Making an inference, consider a song written in 3/4 with three quarter notes in a measure. Now suppose it is written in 3/8 with three eighth notes in a measure, both performed at the same tempo. Would you say "ta ta ta" for the first and "ti ti ti" for the second? Does that make sense to a young child? How do teachers deal with that issue?

IV: Pedagogy

von Laban Yes, what about that?

Kodály That detail troubled others, just as similar problems arose when French syllables were used. I notice, however, some Kodály teachers, and, I believe a minority of Orff teachers as well, now convert to syllables based on beat functions within meters rather than time values of notes.

von Laban What is the difference between the two?

Kodály As I understand it, there are three inseparable parts to rhythm: macrobeats, microbeats, and rhythm patterns. In duple meter, using 2/4, a rhythm pattern of two quarter notes, macrobeats, would be "du du;" two eighth notes, microbeats, would be "du de;" and four sixteenth notes, divisions, would be "du ta de ta." A rhythm pattern of two underlying macrobeats might be "du ta de ta du." Notice, regardless of note values, macrobeats are always "du;" microbeats, "de;" and divisions of microbeats "ta."

In triple meter, say 6/8, two dotted quarter notes, macrobeats as in duple meter, would be "du du;" three eighth notes, microbeats, would be "du da di;" and six sixteenth notes, divisions, would be "du ta da ta di ta." A rhythm pattern of two underlying macrobeats might be "du ta da ta di ta du." Despite note values, macrobeats are always "du;" microbeats, "da di;" and divisions of microbeats "ta."

I hope that placates objections to rhythm solfege and convinces you of the value of rhythm syllables compared to note values. No doubt, in time there will be more innovations and maybe even improvements in rhythm solfege.

von Laban Please tell us about stick notation.

Kodály The idea is to allow students to center on rhythm notation without being encumbered by staff tonal notation. Students see vertical lines and sticks that note heads rest on, but not note heads. Some lines are attached with beams, ligatures if you will, and others are not. Reading is therefore simplified when the tonal dimension is added.

Suzuki I'm confused. If Kodály syllables are based upon note values, don't students need to see rhythm notation to know what syllables to use? If so, is that not an illogical reversal of tonal instruction? Students hear and learn to recite tonal syllables before they see notation. You are saying with rhythm, the reverse is true. What would Pestalozzi say about that?

Kodály I can only say using rhythm syllables based on beat functions solves the problem you raise. I, like Carl Seashore, was a pioneer. Thinking becomes clearer with time and experience. Rhythm solfege is no less valuable than tonal solfege. May we leave it at that?

von Laban I would think use of Kodály syllables would be acceptable after one can read rhythm notation. Is that not correct? If, however, students can already read rhythm, of what merit are syllables? Is not the principle function of rhythm syllables to teach reading?

Kodály Your point would be well taken, Rudolf, if reading were a lone goal. Syllables also teach students to listen with musical meaning. Neology supports that understanding with the coining of the word "audiation."

von Laban That word, "audiation," again.

Kodály Is there anything misguided about it? As indicated heretofore, I anticipate the word will soon come under scrutiny.

Orff I certainly could be wrong, but it seems to me I have come across a form of the word before. It pertained to literature. I believe it was a footnote in the book, The Solace of Hearing by Joyce Coleman. It is reported therein that W. F. Bolton coined "audiate" to describe aural audiences' quite remarkable facility for maintaining their attention and grasping matters of details or overall linguistic structures.

von Laban Zoltán. Have you forgotten hand signs?

Kodály Not at all. Hand signs are an augmentation of Sarah Glover's work. They are a means for individualizing, visualizing, and physically representing tonal syllables. Each pitch is given a unique sound and sign, all relating to a tonic. That is, hand signs give each note a personality in relation to a tonic.

Suzuki Two questions. First, are there hand signs for note values, meaning relative durations, and second, might I be correct to infer visual hand signs are simply another form of reading?

Kodály Infer what seems plausible to you. Kodály instructors are adamant in their belief about hand signs improving intonation. If nothing else, hand signs assist students to sing in tune. I have not, nor do I believe anyone else has, given thought to the notion hand signs might contribute to rhythm achievement.

Jaques-Dalcroze Intonation! If your flat, you're out of tune, but if you sharp, you are expressive.

Corybant My brain has been twisted out of shape, a tad conflicted. I've been granted intoxicating mental stimulation. I need a break and I suppose you do, too. I must restate, however, something Zoltán said before we separate. If I remember correctly, with regard to hand signs, his thought was, each pitch is given a unique sound and sign in relation to a tonic. Upon our return, should we turn that idea inside out, or have you other wishes? Émile and Rudolf would opt for vetting movement, and we must not overlook creativity and/or improvisation. By the way, are they the same or different?

Suzuki Individualized instruction must in no way be waylaid.

Orff By no means am I, nor would I think either Zoltán or Shinicki, have finished exploring classroom pedagogy. There is so much more to compare. Shinicki, we need to get a grip on your approach to, or should I say method for, teaching instrumental music. Were you influenced by Pestalozzi? And, personally, I am far from satisfied with the limited time devoted to rhythm and movement.

Corybant That's enough for the moment.

V:
Movement and Dance

Corybant I'm delighted to see you all again. I apologize for being tardy. Cybele summoned me to assist in some imperative matters. My first responsibility is, of course, to her.

    Have we collective agreement on our next topic?

Jaques-Dalcroze We agree rhythm is fundamental to music education as well as to a general understanding of music. Nevertheless, we have skirted around rhythm. And, what is fundamental to rhythm? Movement, of course. I did not say dance, I said movement. I hope the word "movement" will be sicpassum, that is, will permeate our entire ponderings.

von Laban Thanks for defining sicpassum.

Orff Èmile, I do not underrate movement, I simply sanction that folk dancing is just as important as folk singing in the music education of children and adults alike.

von Laban Carl, dance is movement, do you not agree? Movement before dance, I say. Movement is learned naturally. Dance is taught, it is rehearsed. To discuss dance before movement would be to gull and hobble an otherwise benign discussion.

    I am last to denigrate dance. I taught and worked with Isadora Duncan, Kurt Jooss, and Lisa Ullmann. No one could respect each and their accomplishments more than I. Their gracefulness and plasticity transcended quotidian life. Not only am I a dancer, I was a director of ballet in Staatsoper, Germany. In 1919, I founded my own dance theatre in Stuttgart, Germany.

I would like to add a credo: Dance is convincing, it reveals a person, and it guides us as we discover another world. Freudians, stand clear!

Orff Do we move, pun intended, immediately to movement, or should we first flesh out the difference between learning and teaching? Is that requisite to understanding the difference between movement and dance?

Mason Let's not make the difference between learning and teaching a crucial issue. A simple statement for the moment may be in order.

I remember when colleges and universities offered methods and techniques courses for prospective teachers. Now it is more common to stress learning, not teaching. Teachers teach students so, in time, students are able to teach themselves. And, one teaching oneself is learning. Inferences and generalizations are sources of true erudition as compared to memorization of facts. Succinctly, teaching is from the outside in, whereas learning is from the inside out. Now, what does all this have to do with movement and dance? No more, in my opinion, than it applies to all types of education. Until teachers understand how students learn, their teaching will be compromised, if not hindered, regardless of method or approach being used. So, please, can we get to movement, from the ordinary to the extraordinary. My interest abounds.

Jaques-Dalcroze Lowell, it is not that easy. Whereas Rudolf and I were heavily involved in both movement and dance, Carl Orff's interest centered on dance. That being the case, where do we begin? If what Rudolf said is persuasive, it might be best to begin with movement. Anyway, is movement, dance, or both being taught in schools these days? Perhaps that should be our guide, or is that a nonsequitur?

Orff I have the impression I am odd man out in this troika, so I will bestride the breach, mend the stricture, and begin the dialogue. I will talk about dance. Then we can give full attention to movement.

I'm sure Èmile and Rudolf will support the concept dance must not be marginalized. Dance and movement naturally coexist, movement, of course, being primary. The two are interdependent and thus, do not signify a dichotomy. Gunild Keetman and I realized there was no alternative to coupling primal movement with music in the development of the Schulwerk curriculum. It would be incongruous for me not to emphasize at the onset the two of us were guided in creating activities for the Orff-Schulwerk Elementare Musikübung by Èmile's and Rudolf's accomplishments. They were able to put some of our thoughts into words and action.

Compared to the underlying hypotheses and concepts attached to movement, folk dancing is incredibly straightforward.

Corybant We're on the cusp of a scintillating exchange, so let's not tarry unnecessarily.

Jaques-Dalcroze That Carl recognized my and Rudolf's endeavors is most gratifying.

Orff I hold to phylogenetic philosophy—rediscovery of evolutionary development—in contrast to ontogenetic philosophy—development of an individual—in the music education of children and adults. My doctrine of immediacy is, "To be humanly sound, we must penetrate deeper into humanity." Our ancestry need not be sought abroad, but in the child within us. The child is the font of music.

Going further, in the beginning was the drum. That is to say rhythm is fundamental, being the basis of music, particularly melody. Then words became inseparable from music and movement. Finally, movement set the stage for dance. Melody was derived from speech, and rhythm from gymnastic and dance movements.

It is clear to me Renaissance and Baroque music has to be the basis of a comprehensive process of music pedagogy. Using speech rhymes, with or without specific meaning, children develop a steady beat and gain a sense of patterns. By singing anhemitonic pentatonic folk songs that naturally incorporate a falling minor third, children acquire a sense of tonal relationships. Only later are major and minor introduced.

Next comes movement, both non-locomotor and locomotor, with special attention given to physical coordination. Soon children engage in body percussion followed by dance. Finally, reassigning what they have internalized, children perform on unpitched and then pitched percussion instruments.

Think of it this way: children explore and imitate, then improvise and experiment. Finally they create. Depending upon the resolve of individual teachers, movement and ear training along with improvisation may in due time become integral parts of the entire natural process. What can be simpler than that?

Jaques-Dalcroze Thank you, Carl. I think we are all ready to discuss the anatomy of movement. Rudolf, will you begin or shall I?

von Laban Èmile, I recall you preceded me, Rudolf Jean-Baptiste Attila von Laban, in our birth events by almost fifteen years. In reverence to age, why don't you begin? I will build upon what you say. Your efforts in part stimulated my inquiries.

Jaques-Dalcroze I began teaching as an instructor in music theory at conservatory in Geneva, Switzerland, in 1892. I was immediately appalled by students' lack of sensitivity and expression, and especially by their deficiencies in rhythm. To offer remedial assistance, I insisted all students beat time with their hands. This eventually led to the development of a sequential process of movements involving the entire body. My rhythmic practice was reduced to a system called, as I have told you, Eurhythmics.

By listening to shifting nuances in music I performed at the piano, students first followed directions and later improvised reactions in their movements. At that time, mere exactitude and rules no longer sufficed. The obedience to intent was, through active discovery and experience in the tradition of Pestalozzi and Rousseau, students would acquire kinesthetic awareness and learn to discriminate slight and gross gradations of duration, rubato, tempo, dynamics, strong and secondary accents, phrasing, and form. Students perfected strength and muscular flexibility. The culminating uncommon experience was plastique animée.

In complete denial of students' achievement and their endorsement of Eurhythmics, my application to have the system introduced as a regular course in conservatory was denied. I promptly resigned my position, and that action ushered in mature recognition of the disappointment and rejection later-life offered.

von Laban Shall I commence with particulars of the structure of movement?

Jaques-Dalcroze One moment, please.

In dissecting physical movement, I identified four dimensions: time, space, energy, and balance in relation to gravity. After dissociating them one from another and analyzing all, I reorganized them into a coherent whole. Finally they formed cohesiveness in terms of interdependency. Then I guided students in how to differentiate among them and use each in a proper musical manner. In that way it became clear to them and to me rhythm cannot be forced onto or into students understanding of music through arithmetic, counting, or notation.

von Laban Interesting. You sourced a paradigm of four generic effort movements. I also documented four, but not all are the same as yours. We both acknowledge time and space, of course, are two, but I divided what you refer to as energy into weight and flow. Each of the four have various subparts. Before we compare notes about the four generic parts, we must talk about what I believe are the two fundamentally vital components: time and space. I feel certain you will not disagree with what I have to say. I will, of course, freely translate German terminology into English.

Time is sustained or separated. Space is indirect or direct. When sustained and indirect efforts are combined, a paragon of free-flowing continuous movement is a natural result. In contrast, when separated and direct efforts are combined, movement becomes time-directed, suggesting a specific tempo. Unfortunately, many music teachers teach time before space. By time I mean counting and evaluating note values. Not only does that promote rushing and slowing tempo, but musical expression becomes restricted.

Space is important primarily because it naturally embraces physical distance. For example, if one moves large muscles in a free-flowing continuous manner and accentuates beats at a very slow tempo, say with simultaneous ictus flicks of both wrists, a feeling of physical distance can be audiated—yes, space as well as sound can be audiated—and tempo can be maintained without specified movement. The same idea is functional, of course, when applied to all tempos. I believe Shinicki had this concept in mind when he guided students in moving violin bows in the air. Internal disposition, not external influence, is central.

Jaques-Dalcroze We have much in common, Rudolf. In continuation of what you have said, I forgot to mention corresponding deep breathing must be coordinated with spatial activities. Though difficult to fathom, movement of any type, but particularly free-flowing continuous movement, improves intonation, improvisation and creativity notwithstanding, as well as gives musical specificity to tempo and meter. Contrast that with teachers instructing students to tap toes, as they say, to keep time. There is no weight involved in toe tapping, only stress. If indeed students have not been guided in engaging in spatial body movement readiness and thus are bereft of a sense of consistency of tempo, it would be better to have students raise and lower heels, because then they will be using weight.

von Laban I believe an ancillary thought is pertinent. Just as body weight is shifted to prepare for a jump, body weight is shifted in an anacrusis to prepare for a crusis. Unless a rhythmic jump is prepared and effected with body weight, audiation and the musical performance of a crusis and a metacrusis become barren. Without feeling for relative weight and ability to shift weight at will, movement will not be sustained appropriately, and without sustained movement, feeling for space and flow is aborted. To engage properly in bound-separated time in musical performance, audiation of unbound sustained free flow is indispensable.

Jaques-Dalcroze Balance, yes, that is what you are talking about, the quintessence of balance.

Mason Rudolf, go on and explain the relationship of time and space.

von Laban When movement is sustained, free-flowing, and continuous, it gives a feeling of space without time. That is good, because without feeling space alone, space cannot serve adequately as a foundation for feeling time. Space can exist without time, but time is dependent on space. Thus, it makes sense audiation of time is superimposed on audiation of space.

Audiation of time without audiation of space interrupts all sense of natural flow, of what I want to say are macrobeats, microbeats, and rhythm patterns, in musical phrasing. When movement is sustained and continuous, that is, when music flows freely, there is a feeling of eternity and infinity that expands time and space.

Mason There must be more. What about the concepts of weight and flow?

von Laban Both weight and flow bear on musical expression and interpretation. Weight is light or strong. Flow is free or bound. For example, marches evoke strong and bound movement suggesting tension, whereas jazz blues elicit light and free movement, prompting ease.

All four effort motions in various combinations play a formidable role in elegant artistic movement. For example, whereas tonal patterns move in irregular linear space toward and away from one or more tonal centers, in dissimilarity, rhythm patterns move in continuous circular space as they relate to number and grouping of underlying beats. Although tempo is allied with straightforward motion, tonal patterns and rhythm patterns are audiated in inexact time.

Jaques-Dalcroze Elegant, Rudolf. Well said! Who would have thought a traveling circus rider, a bicycle racer, and amateur painter would fashion such profound insights?

von Laban Good things evolve from bad happenings. Perhaps being injured while dancing in performance pointed my attention toward an analytical direction and introduced me to kinetography. One hardly catches sight of a dancer's movement, a ballet without music. No matter how powerful and magnificent, movement disappears into ether unless it is written in notation, as with literature and music.

Orff There's always more than meets the eye.

Jaques-Dalcroze Rudolf, it has been my experience appropriate movement activities must be initiated with students as early as possible, certainly before age nine. After that time, pseudo sophistication and recognition of the opposite sex sets in and children, boys in particular, become too embarrassed to participate. Also, free-flowing continuous movement should be non-locomotor before locomotor, and large muscle movement should precede small muscle movement. The later is especially true when a student learns to play a music instrument.

von Laban All is good and common sense.

Jaques-Dalcroze In passing, an analogy might be helpful. I assume you know computers have become a citadel in human life.

Corybant Everyone knows about computers. Even in hell.

Jaques-Dalcroze Think of it this way. The human brain is like a computer hard drive. It stores information it receives from software. Without software input, the hard drive is dormant. Body movement may be thought of as the software that informs the brain about tempo and movement.

Physical sensations in the body are transmitted to the brain. In other words, to develop emotions and comprehensive musical understanding, first we feel the body moving, then we cognitively imagine movement of tension and relaxation kinesthetically, and finally, with practical understanding, we return to real movement of the body. To go directly to the brain by counting and reading music notation and thus, skipping spatial activities by circumventing body movement, is ill-advised. Reciting note values is demonstrates information about music, but audiating durations is knowing music.

von Laban I, too, will express a few additional words and then retreat to listening. I have spoken about time, space, weight, and flow, in that order. In movement and music education for adults, that sequence thoughtlessly may seem to make sense, but that order and sequence defies good judgment when applied especially to the music education of young children as well as to older students.

Specifically, it is imperative when working with young children the chain be reversed. Newborns first, and naturally, explore flow, then weight, next space, and only then, time. That process should be followed and complemented in informal and formal music education as young children take on age and become school students. And, I leave you with an undeniable fact. Tempo markings in a music score relate to space, not time. For example, consider the word "largo." It literally means a large area—space— not a slow tempo—time.

Corybant Some of you have mentioned your desire to make personal inquiries of others in the group, and such exchanges may not be suited to public audience. I understand and must admit that kind of information does not interest me. However, may I suggest we give ourselves time to be alone to think and perhaps engage privately with others in the type of conversation some of you have suggested.

Be careful, please, of sensitive intrusions. Tread lightly if you intend to make reference to Rudolf's disappointment when, because of political issues, Goebbels, propaganda minister for the Nazis, with eristic intent, banned a performance of 1,000 singers and dancers Rudolf prepared for the 1936 Berlin Olympics. The fact he worked in German factories before and during World War I to assist in the war effort was disregarded.

It is worthy of note that by analyzing consonance and dissonance in body movement, Rudolf was able to abolish assemblers' unnecessary body action and thus, increase product output in factories. Constructive movements replaced workers' wasted energy in what Rudolf calls shadow movements. Rudolf was wise to immigrate to England in 1937. Be aware, Carl Orff and Dorothee Guenther, under the auspices of the Guetherschule, did design and execute the opening ceremony of music and dance for the 1936 Olympics in Berlin.

von Laban Corybant. You have compelled me to speak again. There is more to the story than you reported. You are much too kind to me. To clear the air, I would like to append some additional information pursuant to my difficulties with the Nazis. My personal spiritual beliefs based on theosophy, Sufism, and Hermeticism will not allow me to disregard the past.

Early on, being so involved with my work and aspirations, I was not as well informed as I should have been about Hitler's intentions. I once wrote, "We want to dedicate our means of expression and the articulation of our power to the service of the great tasks of our Volk. With unswerving clarity our Fuehrer points the way." Moreover, unconscionable as it now seems, in 1933 I was removing all non-Aryan pupils from the children's ballet course I was directing. When reality set in, I was so guilt ridden that I dissociated myself from Nazi agendas. I will forever rue my earlier actions. Allowing such imprudent cooption was, among other relevant issues, the crucible that forced me to leave Germany and take up residence in England.

Forgive me for shocking you. Not intending to further burden you with personal culpability, should you have the inclination, you can read details of what I related in the following two sources: First, "Meister und Werk in der Tanzkunst," Deutsche Tanzzeitschrift, May, 1936, quoted in Horst Koegler, National Socialism, edited by Karl Corino, Hamburg: Hoffman and Campe, 1980, page 176, and second, Hitler's Dancers: German Modern Dance and the Third Reich, Lillian Karina and Marion Kant, translated by Jonathan Steinberg, New York and Oxford, Berghahn Books, 2003.

Orff Rudolf, thank you for your openness and honesty. I, too, have a story to tell regarding my life in Germany during World War II, but, given my mood, this is neither time nor place. While my account is similar in some respects to yours but quite different in others, I remained, in cheerless surroundings, in Munich, Germany, throughout the war.

von Laban It should be noted Zoltán also was not exempt from the contretemps and maliciousness of the Nazis. Performance of his *Peacock Variations* was banned in all conquered territories.

Corybant Rudolf and Carl, I am nonplussed. I had no expectation of this sort of veridical outpouring. I and your colleagues in this colloquium have compassion for both of you. We may think we know what our actions would have been under circumstances similar to yours, but not one of us knows for sure how we would have behaved and fared in the situation. All of us have our own tales veiled in bottomless closets that might be told. But, the past is past, and even God cannot change history.

Seashore True, God cannot change history, but historians can.

VI: Preparatory Audiation and Audiation

Suzuki Corybant, before you convene this session I would like to submit a request. The word "audiation" has been used in several contexts, and I have inferred it might be contrary in meaning to imitation. That being the case or not, a relevant discussion, in my opinion, is mandatory at this juncture. Imitation, you may know, is an integral part of my teaching procedure. It seems I may be missing something. I need to know more about audiation.

Corybant I empathize with your wish. Let's trace that course.

Mason I support having a discussion of the topic. But may we consider preparatory audiation as well as audiation? As I have read, preparatory audiation is related, but not restricted, to developmental music aptitude.

Corybant Who will begin?

Mason Frankly, Corybant, I'm not sure anyone in the group is informed enough. I suggest you, who has gone directly to the source and culled from the book, Learning Sequences in Music: A Contemporary Music Learning Theory, is best able to inform us. I understand the ideas it contains are relatively recent and thus, came shortly after all seven of our lives on earth.

Corybant I can only repeat what I have read, adumbrating what I believe to be central to an understanding of preparatory audiation and audiation itself.

Though preparatory audiation is primary to audiation, from a cursory examination of the two, it appears sensible to begin with audiation. Please understand my hesitation. I am learning, too. I anticipate I will be holding forth for a lengthy time even though I do not intend to outline the types and stages of audiation. Here is what I believe to be a close analysis of what I have learned.

Sound itself is not music. Sound becomes music through audiation, when, as with language, we translate sound in the mind and give it meaning. Meaning given to these sounds will be different depending on the occasion, as well as different from meaning given them by different persons. Audiation is the process of assimilating and comprehending, not simply rehearing, music just heard performed or heard performed sometime in the past. We also audiate when we assimilate and comprehend in our minds music we may or may not have heard, but rather, are reading in notation, composing, or improvising.

Suzuki What is the difference between audiation and aural perception?

Corybant Aural perception takes place when we are actually hearing sound the moment it is being produced. We audiate sound only after we have aurally perceived it. In aural perception we are responding to immediate sound events, whereas in audiation we reconstruct in our minds a past musical event without its sound being physically present. We may audiate when listening to, recalling, performing, interpreting, creating, improvising, reading, or writing music. Though it may seem contradictory, we can listen to and at the same time audiate music.

As analogy, you automatically are thinking now about what I have said while you are listening to what I am saying. It is also possible for you to participate in conversation as you are thinking about what has already been said and might be said. Listening to and participating in a music performance with comprehension, in terms of audiation, and listening to and participating in a conversation with comprehension, in terms of thinking, involve similar operations.

Mason May I interpret? Music and language are different, but they are learned analogously. Am I essentially understanding the concept?

Corybant Yes. Consider language, speech, and thought. Language is the result of need to communicate. Speech is the way we communicate. Thought is what we communicate. Music, performance, and audiation have parallel meanings. Music is the subject of communication. Performance is the vehicle for communication. Audiation is what is communicated.

Although it is said music is not a language primarily because it does not have a grammar, the process appears to be the same for audiating and giving meaning to music as for thinking and giving meaning to speech. When listening to speech, you are giving meaning to what was just said by recalling and making connections with what you heard on earlier occasions. At the same time, you are anticipating or predicting what you will be hearing next based on experience and understanding.

Similarly, when listening to music, you are giving meaning to what you just heard by recalling music you heard on earlier occasions. At the same time, you are anticipating familiar music or predicting unfamiliar music you will be hearing next based on music aptitude and music achievement. In other words, when audiating as you are listening to music, you are summarizing and generalizing content in the context you just heard as a way to anticipate or predict the music that will follow. Every action becomes an interaction. What you are audiating depends on what you have audiated. As audiation develops, it becomes broader and deeper, and thus reflects on itself.

Orff Is this information supported by experimental research?

Corybant Experimental research? I think not. As I recall, it is based on empirical teacher-observer research blended with unanticipated indirect findings derived from experimental investigations on the development and validation of music aptitude and achievement tests. Carl, do you know of any experimental research that explains how we think, that is, how we give meaning to language?

Orff No.

Corybant Experimental research results that explain how we audiate are just as difficult to come by as understanding the process of linguistic comprehension. Perhaps with advances in understanding how brain neurons are clustered, we will have objective evidence that explains psychological as well as physical processes of thinking and audiating.

Mason Please go on.

Corybant Audiation, as opposed to imitation, which is the preliminary step in developing audiation potential, are often confused. Imitation, or what some of us call inner hearing, is a product, whereas audiation is a process. It is possible, and unfortunately too often the case, to perform a piece of music by imitation without engaging in audiation. It is not possible, however, to imitate and audiate at the same time. Learning by rote is not the same as learning with understanding, whether the subject be history, mathematics, or music. Imitation is learning through someone else's ears. Audiation is learning through one's own ears. Imitation becomes particularly problematic when it slides into memorization. As memorization becomes stronger, audiation becomes weaker.

Kodály Corybant, are you suggesting what you have read postulates audiation and inner hearing as being different?

Corybant Yes. As I grasp it, one can inner hear without musically understanding what is being heard. Persons may remember a song or etude, that is, inner hear it, but not know, for example, whether it is in major or minor, duple or triple, or its harmonic structure. Believe it or not, there is research that reveals when asked to stop performing in the middle of a simple song or extended composition, some professional and many amateur players cannot sing the resting tone or produce it instrumentally without consulting the notation in front of them. They may be inner hearing, but assuredly they are not audiating.

Kodály That is no surprise.

Corybant I will conclude with what might be thought of as an infinitesimal, but nonetheless significant, addendum.

Audiation of music notation is called notational audiation. Just as aural perception is different from audiation, so the process of decoding notation is different from notational audiation. If you give meaning to what you see in music notation by silently hearing its musical sound before you or someone else performs it instrumentally, you are engaging in notational audiation. Also, if you create and notate music without consulting a music instrument, again, you are engaging in notational audiation. Too often and lamentably, one reads or writes notation without audiating the sounds it represents. When that occurs, the person is simply decoding symbols—individual written notes—and is not conscious of the content of the patterns or context that constitute the music.

Suzuki We should have undertaken this discussion long before now. It is clear to me the thrust of what has been reported as imitation is requisite for learning to audiate. However, I wonder if a common pedagogical fallacy is not to assist students in crossing the bridge from imitation to audiation. That may be akin to repeating a sentence in a foreign language without understanding the message, or by simply copying words letter-by-letter, that is, deciphering them, on a alphabetical keyboard.

Mason What do books report about preparatory audiation?

Corybant Children are guided through three types of tonal and rhythm preparatory audiation. They are acculturation, imitation, and assimilation. Further, there are three stages of preparatory audiation within the acculturation type, two within the imitation type, and two within the assimilation type.

Just as children engage in speech babble vocalization before they learn to speak the language of their culture, so children in the developmental music aptitude stage engage in music babble vocalization. From birth to about eighteen months, when children are in the initial stage of music babble, they develop subjective language and subjective tonal and rhythm contexts. When approximately eighteen months old, they begin to use objective language and music contexts, and so begin to rely less and less on subjective language and subjective music context. During that time, children say what they are thinking as they are thinking it, and they sing what they are hearing as they are hearing it. When older, they begin to conceptualize, and so think before they speak and audiate before they sing. Yet, their behavior before age three is fundamental to later achievement, because the basis for creativity and improvisation is embedded in early subjective thinking and subjective audiation.

Early in the music babble stage, a child learns to deal with the aural and the oral separately, and that provides readiness for combining the two.

Kodály Is it reasonable to assume what you have said correspondingly applies to older students as well as children?

Corybant It would seem so. With regard to children, however, I was not amazed to learn a child may emerge from tonal and rhythm babble stages at the same time or at different times. Children who have initially emerged from music babble are able to distinguish, practically, not theoretically, of course, between major and harmonic minor tonalities, and between usual duple and usual triple meters. However, they usually remain in the music babble stage in terms of other tonalities and meters. That is, children who are in the developmental music aptitude stage may or may not have emerged entirely from music babble. It is believed even though children may have high developmental music aptitude, they cannot be forced out of music babble any sooner than they themselves choose. If a child is forced out of music babble, he or she may seek autism as a refuge.

Orff Returning to preparatory audiation, I am delighted with what Corybant has related. It has always been my belief teaching should not be for the child but from the child's viewpoint. Likewise, in regard to audiation, sequential learning in Orff-Schulwerk posits the imitation of patterns as readiness for improvisation in its overall structure. The concept of notational audiation is supported by the fact children are capable of and enjoy inventing their own system of notation. It seems much of what I intuited is verified by contemporary empirical research.

Suzuki "Education" and "instruction," are the key contrasting words. In the Talent Education Institute in Japan, singing is taught concurrently with imitation. What is imitated vocally is conveyed to the music instrument. All students must learn to sing, whether or not instrumental study is planned. Both Carl Orff and Èmile have attested to this central component of music education. I trust all this is agreed upon. However, I feel somewhat goaded by the denigration of memorization. Of course, memory plays an important role in imitation as well as audiation, but so does memorization. Isn't that the way students learn language?

Mason Not completely. I cannot deny memorization of the multiplication table has merit. But Shinicki, think about it. Most of what you know you did not memorize, or for that matter, read. I indulged students in memorization, but I'm not sure that was a good approach, particularly for learning music. Let me explain.

I have read we have various language vocabularies, and I will identify them in sequential order in terms of their development. Ideally, there are five vocabularies: listening, speaking, thinking, reading, and writing. Of the five parallel music vocabularies, the first and largest is listening, then performing, then audiation and improvisation, then reading, and finally writing. However, with age, the reading vocabulary, not surprisingly, becomes as large or larger than the performing vocabulary. Note, however, without large and comprehensive listening, performing, and audiation and improvisation vocabularies, students have little chance of acquiring even limited music reading and writing vocabularies.

Remember, the audiation vocabulary is to music what the thinking vocabulary is to language. In language, we stop imitating when we are able to think and speak familiar words and ask and answer questions. In music, we stop imitating when we are able to audiate and perform patterns to conceive music of our own choosing. The third vocabularies in thinking and music are predicated upon creativity and improvisation. It would be unconscionable not to expect children to develop a thinking vocabulary. However, it appears to be acceptable to many music educators for persons to go through life without even attempting to develop an audiation vocabulary.

Suzuki Lowell, you know perhaps better than I change is difficult. My adherents have enjoyed great success teaching according to principles I have laid down over the years. Unconscious memorization is a crucial component of Suzuki teaching. I fear what the outcome might be if memorization were to be censured.

Mason Shinicki, as you give thought to what Corybant has related, might you consider how a beneficial transition, crossing the bridge, as has been said, might be made from imitation to audiation, and if you solve that issue, you possibly might discover emphasis on memorization to be unwarranted. For example, is it possible to memorize unconsciously? Be assured, I'm not seeking your immediate response.

Kodály May I offer a quotation from John Keat's Ode on a Grecian Urn? "Heard melodies are sweet, but those unheard are sweeter."

Corybant I think we have currently gone as far as we profitably can with audiation. Are we ready to change the subject? I have not forgotten two topics we have bypassed or my promise to revisit both. Namely, individual differences and the development of the musical ear vertically rather than horizontally. Remember, it was suggested good intonation is consummated by linking pitches to a resting tone rather than melodically to one another, as in traditional interval training.

Talk about change, can you imagine the fulmination and ruckus that might emerge among music theorists if memorizing names of intervals from a minor second to a major seventh were abandoned? I'm beginning to think naming and hearing intervals is much ado about nothing. Constant audiation of a resting tone may be all that need be taught, or should I say learned. Èmile, I sense you, for one, disagree. Good, that should provide for future substantive discussion.

VII: More Pedagogy

Corybant What a wild night! I don't remember telling you, maybe I did, Cybele is the Phrygian goddess of nature. She was traveling and became tired, and I can understand why. Group frenzied, exotic dancing amid consumption of spirits takes its toll. She located me and unabashedly demanded I act as her companion on her return trip to the realm above Asia Minor, her home. Of course, I acquiesced. Upon our arrival, we, among a circle of her cult, celebrated Cybele as earth mother. I am simply exhausted.

Orff Are you well enough to participate?

Corybant My acumen is far from nil. I'm ready for further reaches.

Kodály Allow me to refresh your memory, Corybant. The two subjects you suggested we discuss are first, teaching to students' individual musical differences and needs, and second, development of the musical ear. We have already talked about solfege and absolute pitch. To what else might you be giving thought, Corybant?

Jaques-Dalcroze I think I know what is occupying Corybant's mind. Let's conclude our discussion about comparative values and limitations of teaching perfect pitch.

Orff Did we agree it could be taught? I don't remember we did.

Jaques-Dalcroze We didn't. However, I claim it should, notice I did not say can, be taught. Students memorize the sound of "C" and then compare that pitch to any other pitch they hear. In that way they recognize and name the sound of every pitch. I call that inner hearing. Students learn to read with their ears and hear with their eyes. Who started this myth about tone deafness?

Suzuki A bad environment can instill tone impairment, if not tone deafness.

Kodály Èmile, I am partial to teaching relative pitch. It has practical value. In Kodàly instruction, we stress the keys of "C," "F," and "G," so in the second year of study, students develop a strong sense of key center.

With regard to what you call perfect pitch, there is a difference between identifying a specific pitch and being able to perform that pitch. They are different attributes. Do you believe if students identify a pitch they will be able to produce it in good intonation regardless of availability of a reference pitch? I do not think that is necessarily a fact. In linkage, I would like to emphasize there is a theoretical difference between the words "recognition" and "identification." In my opinion, the former exudes primacy in music education.

Orff What is the difference between recognition and identification?

Kodály We recognize something familiar, but identify something unfamiliar on the basis of being knowledgeable of similar familiar objects or ideas.

Mason For the sake of discussion, let us agree perfect pitch can be taught. That being the case, absolute pitch could prove to be more a handicap that an asset. For example, "F#" in the key of "D" sounds different when it is the leading tone in the key of "G." Moreover, a pitch at the beginning of a phrase usually subjectively, if not objectively, sounds different when in the middle or end of a phrase.

Also, in extension of the subject of pitch, I suggest a perfect fourth, for example, sounds different when heard in different parts of a scale. "So do" sounds different from "do fa" contextually, but both, nonetheless, are ascending perfect fourths. I don't think perfect pitch

VII: More Pedagogy

ameliorates that situation; it only aggravates it. Èmile, by insisting on perfect pitch, you may be anchoring students in technique at the expense of musical sensitivity. Both, of course, are important, but it would be unconscionable not to pay homage to the latter.

Suzuki We have used the words "content" and "context" throughout our deliberations without defining them. I think an understanding of the two words is essential. As I think I understand the percept, and I hope I'm not being simplistic, context refers to mode—for example, major, minor, Dorian, Mixolydian, and so on. Content refers to collections of pitches in that mode—for example, a major tonic tonal pattern, "CEG," or a major dominant tonal pattern, "GBD." In rhythm, context refers to meter, for example, duple or triple. Content refers to collections of durations, for example, a rhythm pattern of two eighth notes followed by a quarter note in duple meter.

That being said, it seems to me individual pitches and durations—content—, have no artistic musical meaning apart from mode and meter—context. And I personally think tonal patterns and rhythm patterns, not single pitches and durations, convey musical meaning, not theoretical understanding associated with perfect pitch or perfect tempo.

Orff What is perfect tempo?

Mason The ability to audiate an exact tempo.

Jaques-Dalcroze Do you prize perfect tempo but not perfect pitch? If so, why?

Mason Not necessarily. I simply answered a question.

Corybant Equanimity, gentlemen. Zoltán, what about vertical and horizontal ear training?

Kodály In traditional ear training classes, regardless of whether a teacher's intent is to teach relative or perfect pitch, students are taught to recognize intervals, such as major and minor seconds, thirds, sixths, and sevenths, as well as perfect, diminished, and augmented fourths, fifths, and octaves. That is, they are taught to read horizontally, one pitch to the next. The anticipation is by familiarizing oneself with names of intervals that move horizontally, good intonation will result.

But this may not be a valid conviction. A supposedly static interval actually changes its shape, if I may use that word, depending upon, as already explained, its position in a scale and where it is heard in a musical passage. Succinctly, I myself have unwaveringly counseled, and what my interpretation of current research results by music psychologists substantiate is, it might be well to teach students to audiate a resting tone, or a tonic if you will, at all times, continuously while performing various pitches melodically.

Audiation of vertical solfege relationships of all ongoing pitches to a prevailing resting tone engenders good intonation. Forcing memorization of and naming horizontal intervals is inessential. It should not be seen as contradictory, however, that I am inclined to continue to follow and bind myself to these research findings. In accretion, they support my belief.

Corybant Now, what about individual musical differences?

Jaques-Dalcroze All of us, as well as any intelligent person who has taught music, know there are enormous differences among students, musical and otherwise. Lowell stressed that early on. Laypersons usually do not understand there is no average student. We as teachers must be in the forefront in shedding light on the often disregarded reality of individual differences. It is imperative teachers acknowledge students are unique and thus, engage in different types of feedback mechanisms to convey information to the mind and body. Teachers who are not alert to this tend to teach as if every student has average musicality. Superior students become bored and inferior students become angry. Both groups can develop negative attitudes toward

VII: More Pedagogy

school music, and later to music in general. Nobody learns much of anything constructive.

Corybant I am somewhat constrained to bring this related topic into play. It has come to my attention approximately 50% of students with overall music aptitude above the 80th percentile—the upper 20%—on valid music aptitude tests do not engage in elective school music activities beyond what might be required in ordinary classroom music. What a waste of effort and human talent. That situation would not be tolerated in terms of students' various levels of intelligence.

Suzuki Why are we focusing on music aptitude? Differences among students are caused by environmental influences. Moreover, may not students' individual musical differences be accounted for by whether they play first chair or sit in subordinate sections.

Mason You are sanctioning the notion teaching practices should be individualized on the basis of music achievement. Shinicki, the correlation between music aptitude and music achievement is about .55, meaning the two have approximately 25% in common. A reprehensible consequence is that many students with high music aptitude receive no music instruction, whereas many with low music aptitude do.

Suzuki With regard to the latter, is that a crime? All students have a right to learn music and, with proper individualized instruction, all can achieve high levels.

von Laban Bravo! I agree. Regardless of gender, educational standing, or social status, all students can learn to dance.

Kodály Yes, and all persons are musical.

Seashore All students have a right to be taught, but not all will or can achieve highest levels.

Jaques-Dalcroze Currently on earth there are gifted and talented programs within some comprehensive schools, as well as others, that solely constitute charter and magnet schools. That is at least an attempt to take students' individual musical differences and needs into account in innovative ways.

It occurs to me, however, given those solutions, the situation may be exacerbated rather than improved, because most administrators do not know the difference between a gifted student and a talented student. Gifted students have high intelligent quotients, this is, IQ's, whereas talented students excel in the arts. Since we are talking about correlation, it should be of interest to know the coefficient describing the relationship between music aptitude and general intelligence is approximately .05. That means they share little more than 2%, if that much, commonality.

Suzuki What's the problem with that?

Jaques-Dalcroze The concern is that not all highly intelligent students are highly musical, and not all highly musical students are highly intelligent. To teach them all together makes no sense. Why? I suspect because administrators are uninformed, or perhaps it is the simplest way for insecure shills to defray parental complaints, or both. I believe gifted and talented programs don't function as intended because assigned teachers are not always gifted or talented.

Seashore I would say the actual reason for failure of most gifted and talented programs is invalid criteria are used to identify students with high musical potential. In many cases, scores on a pencil and paper test of theoretical knowledge and a record of taking music lessons are relied upon rather than musical promise. Isn't it the neighborhood piano teacher, anyway, who is most influential and usually gives the subjective nod for a student to be accepted into a gifted and talented program? Forgive them, for they know not what they do.

von Laban I recall a hapless music critic who was assigned to review a recital given by one of limited musical means. His comment was, "When playing the piano, the performer depressed the keys as well as those who unfortunately were forced to listen."

Mason Music teachers have so much fear of music aptitude tests.

Seashore Well, some music teachers are apprehensive about possibly being asked to take a music aptitude test themselves. As I have implied heretofore, music teachers' average total score on a valid music aptitude test parks somewhere below the upper third in terms of percentile norms.

Corybant I believe it is an apposite time to adjourn this session.

VIII: Music Achievement and Grading

Mason If I remember correctly, music aptitude was the central topic of our initial conversation. I assumed at the time it was a natural harbinger of a discussion about music achievement, which has not yet come to pass. Might this be an appropriate time to introduce that vitally important, but nonetheless too often neglected, subject?

Seashore Lowell, are you interested primarily in measuring music achievement or evaluating music achievement?

Suzuki What's the difference between measurement and evaluation?

Seashore Measurement typically addresses techniques for examining students' music achievement, whereas evaluation centers on teachers' routines of interpreting students' derived measures of achievement and then reporting their resultant opinions and grades to parents and professionals.

Mason It would seem determination of grades is a subjective matter. What about measurement?

Seashore The word "measurement" signifies dimensions, quantity, or capacity compared to a standard. Thus, it is necessarily objective. Nonetheless, levels of students' achievement may be subjectively appraised, and that is common practice in music education. When that is the case, measurement, of course, is sidestepped as a basis upon which evaluations should be established.

Orff Most music teachers have not been taught measurement techniques. Isn't that why they evaluate students without benefit of measurement?

Mason Indeed it is a significant contributing factor.

Orff Why isn't instruction in measurement a staple in music teacher education?

Seashore Good question?

Mason I can understand why evaluation without measurement serving as a guide may not appear to be problem. After all, persons habitually marry, join a church, vote, and make purchases without benefit of measurement. Ad hominem reference and tradition loom large.

von Laban I'm told the divorce rate in the United States of America is moving above 50%, and counting. May we attribute that malaise of evaluation to a lack of measurement?

Jaques-Dalcroze May I add to such ludicrousness by asking how one might call upon measurement for guidance when choosing a spouse?

von Laban Carl Seashore, have you ever given thought to writing a love aptitude test?

Corybant Enough foolishness. May we satisfy Lowell's request by bringing music achievement to the fore?

Seashore Yes. But, first, I am compelled to say it is possible to create tests of music achievement, tests that measure both musical skills and knowledge.

Jaques-Dalcroze An aptitude test for love is deemed impossible. However, I'm sure there are some among us who are able to rise to the occasion and write a valid test of love achievement.

VIII: Music Achievement and Grading

Corybant Rudolf, your amusement is contagious, but again I say, enough! Let's get on with it. Carl Seashore, please lead the way.

Seashore All tests are measures, but not all measures are tests. You know what tests are, but perhaps you're in a quandary about the nature of a measure that is not a test. A good example is a rating scale. Whereas pencil and paper music achievement tests are designed to measure theoretical and historical knowledge about music, rating scales seem to be the optimal alternative for measuring students' instrumental music and vocal performance achievement.
 Shall I discuss tests or rating scales first?

von Laban Wait! Cannot rating scales also be used for measuring students' movement achievement?

Seashore Of course, and I would think it would be you, Rudolf and Émile, who are best qualified to write the content of such rating scales.

Jaques-Dalcroze Carl, would you care to elucidate the process of writing content for rating scales?

Seashore Yes. Shall I begin there or with test construction?

Kodály Let's discuss tests first.

Seashore As for aptitude tests, reliability and validity of achievement tests must be investigated regardless of whether they are teacher-made, that is, written by teachers in the schools, or authored by professionals and made available by publishers. It is expected published tests will be standardized. Standardized tests are administered and scored in a prescribed established manner, and norms are provided in teacher guides for using the tests.

Orff Carl, a short explanation of norms might be helpful.

Mason Let me attempt that. Consider an average score on a test is 32. Now suppose a student's score is 40. The obvious question is whether 40 is meaningfully superior to 32, and if so, how much? That query is answered by an examination of normative comparisons among students' scores.

For example, if few students obtain scores of 40, 40 may be considered quite high. On the other hand, if a sufficient number of students score above 40, that score is not so impressive. Norms for most tests are reported in terms of percentile ranks, which range from 1 to 99. A percentile rank is a standard score, that is, it may be interpreted with standard meaning on any test as being from exceptionally high to extremely low. A percentile rank of 60, for example, means a student's score is as high or higher than 60% and lower than 40% of students who took the test. Carl Seashore has spoken of standard scores.

Jaques-Dalcroze Are we ready to discuss test content?

Kodály Test content is a matter of test validity. Students should be tested on what they have been directly and indirectly taught. Thus, content of a test is a reflection of a curriculum. Without a curriculum that comprises teaching objectives to serve as a guide, test questions, that is, test content, can be expected to be unfocused.

Orff Are you suggesting teachers should teach to a test?

Seashore No. What is being said is that a test is best written after a curriculum is developed and instruction has taken place. In that event, teaching to the test would appear improbable.

Orff You don't believe students should be expected to memorize answers and iterate information, do you?

Seashore I hope not. Carl, a test comprises test questions that ask students both to demonstrate verbatim what they have memorized and to make inferences. Think of it this way. With regard to inferences, students are taught information about A and B, and on the test they are challenged to make use of that knowledge to generalize an answer for a question pertaining to C, a question for which specific information has not been taught. To me, inclusion of inference-making questions epitomizes a sterling test. Generalization, as I have implied, is the core, if not the soul, of learning.

Jaques-Dalcroze Writing an essay question of that type is not an easy matter.

Mason No it is not, so why concern yourself with an essay test, which supposedly teaches students to write as well as to impart learned information. If you want students to learn to use the written language, first teach them how to speak and then assign an essay for them to write.

von Laban What kind of an examination might you suggest if not an essay?

Seashore A multiple-choice test.

Orff I should have expected that answer from an American. European professors sit with a student, one-on-one, and ask the student questions. Certainly the professor is capable of knowing whether a student passes or fails.

Mason I shudder to think of reliability of such an examination, validity notwithstanding.

Seashore Essay tests are easy to write but difficult to score. Multiple-choice tests are difficult to write but undemanding to score. The former type engenders evaluation void of measurement, whereas the latter type ensures measurement, which, in turn, decreases to a great extent bias and enhances precision in evaluation.

Kodály I'm familiar with the term "normative grading," but what is idiographic grading?

Mason I, too, have come across those terms in reading. I think I can explain the difference. In normative grading, students are compared to one another. In idiographic grading, a student is compared to himself or herself. In an idiographic analysis, a student's achievement may be compared to his or her aptitude or former achievement. In my opinion, information the normative approach provides is best for teachers and administrators, whereas idiographic information is, without question, more beneficial than norms, if not vital, for students and parents. In fact, an idiographic analysis is key for appropriately teaching to students' individual differences and needs.

Corybant All this is interesting, but I would like to extend the nucleus of the topic. Are grades primarily for students or teachers? Yes, I know, it is important for various reasons for students and parents to be informed of current achievement, but I would think teachers could benefit as much, if not more, from such knowledge. It not only tells them how well they are teaching but more importantly, it guides them in establishing new objectives for ongoing advanced teaching.

Seashore Yes, and that is most advantageously accomplished by continuous measurement, perhaps week-by-week, in contrast to end-of-the semester or yearly testing.

Corybant There are other issues I would like to have resolved. As I read, more often than not I see the words "pretest" and "post test" used in association with research and measuring students' academic growth. What does pretesting and post testing have to do with assessing students' achievement?

Mason Before we enter that discussion, I want to respond to Corybant's use of the word "assessment." It recently has been introduced as a euphemism for evaluation by professors and teachers who don't understand measurement processes. It is intended to accommodate unaware parents as well as to excuse and give uninformed teachers permission not to use measurement as a necessary concomitant of evaluation. To assess is to estimate, and to estimate student's achievement bears on straight-ahead subjective evaluation with objectivity disregarded. I myself choose not to use the word.

Corybant Carl Seashore, are you cognizant of pretesting and post testing?

Seashore Yes. Early on, educators studied an agricultural research model to investigate objective change. For example, investigators establish comparability of the soil of two fields in a pretest, use different fertilizers, seed both, and then compare the yield of the two fields at the end of the growing season in a post test to determine if one fertilizer is more productive than the other. Medical doctors use pretests and post tests in a similar manner to discover if a new drug is more effective than a placebo.

Educators adopted the pretest-post test model to research change in student achievement. In time it became apparent that model for studying physical change is inappropriate for studying cognitive change. The reason is the same achievement test cannot be administered both as a pretest and a post test because, given proper instruction, it is either too difficult as a pretest or too easy as a post test. In both cases, scores lack variability and thus, reliability approaches zero, indicating the test is invalid for its intended purpose or purposes.

Kodály Carl, are you saying music aptitude tests but not music achievement tests are valid?

Seashore Certainly not. Different tests, not the same test, should be used to test music achievement. A test designed with appropriate content as a pretest and another with different appropriate content as a post test is the solution. Current researchers refer to this as multi-level testing.

Corybant Carl, I interpret what you have said to mean it is possible to investigate cognitive change but not cognitive growth.

Seashore Bravo! Yes, and I wish music education researchers would acknowledge that fact.

Suzuki But suppose I want to investigate growth in music achievement of my students. Can I do that?

Seashore Yes, indirectly. The only way I understand that it can be done reasonably is to compare percentile ranks on two tests. If a student achieves the same or nearly the same percentile rank on both tests, it may be assumed normal growth is taking place. It is obvious a decrease or increase in percentile ranks indicates otherwise.

Kodály Of course, isn't that the way it is done in reading, spelling, and arithmetic? I can't imagine the same test in those subjects being repeatedly administered at the beginning and end of the year, or from grade-to-grade.

Suzuki I'm anxious for relevant information to be put forward about rating scales. As I recall, Carl Seashore said they are the best, if not the only, vehicle for objectively measuring performance achievement. Carl, I would appreciate your introducing the topic.

Seashore Again, I begin with reliability and validity. For a rating scale to have practical value, it must be reliable, and as with tests, it cannot be valid unless it is reliable. Remember, however, because a test or rating scale is reliable in no way guarantees it is valid. Further research is necessary to establish its validity.

Research indicates a rating scale should have more than one dimension with five sequential criteria in each dimension. Dimensions may be tonal, rhythm, and expression. Consider a short major etude in common time. The criteria for the rhythm dimension may be 1) maintains a consistent tempo, 2) sustains the established meter, 3) performs quarter and eighth notes correctly, 4) performs division patterns correctly, and 5) performs elongation patterns correctly.

VIII: Music Achievement and Grading

von Laban I can guess what a division pattern is, sixteenth notes, for example, but what is an elongation pattern?

Kodály An elongation pattern might be a dotted or half note or tied notes. But what about rests and upbeats?

Suzuki It is more difficult to reveal musicianship when playing slow rather than fast.

Seashore Remember, I indicated criteria should be sequential, from 1 to 5, with 5 being the highest level of achievement. Using a continuous rating scale, a student cannot be awarded a 2 unless he or she attains a 1, a 3 unless a 2, and so on. That goes a long way in ensuring sufficient reliability and validity. Use of sequential criteria suggests the teacher is following a viable curriculum. Furthermore, use of numbers without designating specific accomplishment is an invitation to questionably low reliability. Numbers suggest the teacher is vague about what is being or has been taught.

Zoltán, depending upon the advancement of students and nature of a curriculum, rests and upbeats may represent higher levels in the rhythm dimension.

Mason I remember seeing vocal and instrumental performance rating scales that awarded points for correct notes and subtracted points for incorrect notes.

Jaques-Dalcroze That's nonsense. If I understand even a bit about music and measurement, such a procedure contributes to high reliability but diminishes validity.

Seashore Correct.

Kodály Patterns, not individual notes, should be the concern.

Suzuki What about technical skills?

Kodály That would call for a separate dimension.

Suzuki All this reminds me of a joke. While playing a long tremolo, one bass player, looking sideways at the bass player sharing his music stand, says, "your rushing."

Jaques-Dalcroze Bass players! A famous conductor once asked the principal bassist in the orchestra if it were possible for bass players to perform more in tune or would the nature of their instrument preclude the possibility?

von Laban It would seem to me that Émile and I left appropriate criteria on earth for movement teachers to write valid rating scales to measure and evaluate effort motions.

Seashore And don't forget, valid rating scales can be composed for measuring and evaluating vocal performance.

Jaques-Dalcroze What about improvisation? It is my opinion the main purpose of teaching music is to guide students in making music their own, and that may be best accomplished through learning to improvise.

Corybant Have we concluded our discussion of music achievement and grading?

Kodály Not quite. There is an issue only touched upon: grading.

Seashore Grading is of highest quality when students are evaluated both normatively and ideographically. Both types of grades might be included on a report card. Further, separate grades in tonal and rhythm achievement, or whatever is central to a curriculum at the time, provide parents and students with important diagnostic information.

Mason It seems clear without a worthy curriculum and valid measurement and evaluation techniques to support what has been said, none of it can become a reality.

Seashore Also, directors of music ensembles—band, orchestra, and chorus—often grant high grades indiscriminately. If grade distributions for a class were included on a report card, interpretation of individual grades would gain precision. If 90% of students were given the highest grade, that grade would be less impressive than if only 10% of students received the grade.

Corybant I declare this session concluded.

IX: Tonal Essentials

Mason It was pleasant having a temporary break. At times I concentrated so strenuously on what was being said, some salient points transcended me. I eagerly anticipate reviewing the transcript of the dialogue conserved by Corybant's aide.

Corybant That will be possible.

Mason I had opportunity to have conversation with Carl Seashore during our recess. I was 74 years old when Carl was born. Thus, I possess information of professional interest to both Carl and me that occurred in the United States of America before he became gripped by music education. It was revitalizing for me to pass on to him events I thought long ago had slipped my mind.

Corybant Tell us about them.

Mason As I have related, in 1832 George J. Webb and I founded the Boston Academy of Music. George authored a music theory text that stimulated profound thinking among collegial musicians. His writing most likely parallels Karl Wilhelm Julius Hugo Riemann's. Mr. Riemann was a professor of musicology and a theoretician at the University of Leipzig, in Germany. He was born in 1849 and died in 1919, his death occurring just about the time Carl's professional celebrity was coming to pass. The professor's writings dominated the thinking of European musicologists who were striving to separate the discipline of music theory from musicology, the later destined to become solely music history, within the academy. Their success and Hugo Riemann's Handbuch der Harmonielehre, published in Leipzig, Germany, in 1887, occupied most of Carl's and my conversation.

Jaques-Dalcroze I heard of Professor Riemann's work.

Mason I will summarize our discussion. Carl, my impression is, whether you are aware or not, Hugo Riemann's writings circuitously influenced the choice of content and the psychological constructs underlying your music aptitude test battery.

You remember the meanings of the words "context" and "content." It is plausible to assume the difference between those concepts was not of importance, if they indeed their bilateral, or may I metaphorically suggest bicameral, nature occurred to musicologists and theoreticians a century or more ago. Music theorists then were preoccupied with individual pitches rather than tonal patterns.

Think about this for a moment. If I asked you to reconstruct silently a simple familiar phrase or melody, you would audiate series of patterns, each comprising on average of two to five contiguous pitches as they relate to a tonal center, not individual disconnected pitches one by one. It is tonal patterns and rhythm patterns, not alphabetic parts of tonal patterns and rhythm patterns, or individual pitches and durations, that constitute music. Patterns are to music what words are to language, and isolated pitches and durations and their names have as little meaning to musical understanding as letters of the alphabet have to linguistic comprehension.

Seashore So, are you saying the subtest of pitch discrimination may not have been a good idea?

Jaques-Dalcroze Correct me if I am wrong, but did not your test of tonal memory require students to listen to a series of three to five pitches twice and then determine which pitch in the series the second time was changed?

Seashore Well, do you not consider a series of pitches a tonal pattern?

Jaques-Dalcroze You might say so, but I thought Lowell indicated content of a tonal pattern had to be associated with context of a tonal center. If students subjectively impose a tonal center on a series of pitches, isn't that, in itself, a measure of music aptitude? If so, why is the test called one of tonal memory rather tonal relationships?

Moreover, some pitch differences on the test were, if I recall correctly, as little as eight cents apart. Considering half steps are one hundred cents apart, is it truly possible a pitch somewhere between the cracks on a keyboard indeed can be related to a tonal center?

Seashore Do you think an instrument can be tuned properly if the tuner cannot discriminate a nominal difference between two pitches?

Orff Can we slow down a bit? I'm hearing too many questions and not enough answers.

Jaques-Dalcroze Only one or two more questions. Carl, would the pitch discrimination test have been better called a test of tonal imagery? And, putting aside minute cent differences, does a student's ability to inner hear a physically non-sounding tonal center guarantee he or she will know which pitch was changed?

Orff Professor Riemann is not at fault for all this nitpicking. Much of this type of academic thinking goes back to the Greeks, if not before.

Corybant Beware of reckless embattlement in search of immaterial issues.

Mason Can it be denied Professor Riemann contributed to that form of theoretical thought? Either way, however, whether he did or not is inconsequential.

Kodály A moment, please. The content and context hypothesis concerns me. I'm thinking specifically about intervals. What has been posited concerning pitch discrimination and tonal memory logically applies to what has been said about vertical and horizontal interval discrimination or recognition.

Mason I would think so.

Kodály Also, I don't understand why we are creating a dichotomy between tonal and rhythm dimensions of music. Melody, the soul of music, combines pitch and rhythm.

Mason Zoltán, don't Kodály teachers teach tonal and rhythm patterns separately?

Kodály Yes, but only in the beginning. They are soon combined. You know, I was indirectly enmeshed in a folklorism-dodecaphony debate. I explained the tonal basis of my music separates it from folk music, and its anhemitonic pentatonic character disunites it from diatonic scales. Nonetheless, tonal and rhythm elements ultimately are combined. Of course, major and minor are introduced later along with other modes.

Orff That is the case with my pedagogy. Pentatonic, excluding semitones, is used initially, and drones, borduns, and ostinati are fundamental as prologue to elemental harmony. When students' music achievement warrants it, major, Aeolian, Dorian, and Phrygian are introduced accordingly. Harmony plays a subordinate role to the interaction of melody, rhythm, and sonority, as in folk music.

Jaques-Dalcroze From my point of view, along with rhythm and dynamics, melody and harmony are inseparable. They are all brought together through improvisation, with the voice as the natural instrument.

Mason Getting back to music aptitude, Carl never called his test of tonal memory a test of musical memory. He was well aware of the substance of his work. Can this matter be settled by accepting the idea there is discrimination ability and musical ability? Carl Seashore said discrimination prowess is indispensable for music achievement.

Kodály Then why, Carl, did you title your test one of musical talent rather than one of requisite musical discrimination skill or auditory acuity?

Orff Hindsight is not twenty-twenty foresight.

Mason I want to propose a thorough examination of tonality.

Jaques-Dalcroze Of course.

Mason As you know, major and minor took on added importance as a result of Johann Sebastian Bach's compositions. Before Bach's birth in 1865, but less so after his death in 1750, the importance of modes, for example, Dorian and Mixolydian, was ubiquitous, certainly in folk music. Bach stabilized major and minor harmonically in contrast to other composer's reliance on flow of melody and counterpoint in more serious works. So, I shall take modes as a starting point.

Around 1900, it became common practice to refer to Dorian, Phrygian, Lydian, Mixolydian, and sometimes Locrian, as modes. Major and minor were barred from that classification. Students were indoctrinated with the belief major and minor are not modes. How unfortunate, because among other consequences, that myth is prevalent today. Truth is, major is the Ionian mode, and minor, the Aeolian mode.

Orff We are aware of this.

Mason Yes, of course. I remind you only to set the stage for what Carl and I discussed. An old word has taken on new, extended, meaning. The word is "tonality." In our time, tonality had an uncomplicated meaning: Loyalty to a tonic, that is, to the key scheme of a composition. Now, key is one thing and tonality another.

Kodály This is entrancing. Go on.

Mason Because a majority of musicians use the word "mode" to mean any scale other than major or minor, the value of the word has been compromised. Thus, "tonality" is currently becoming the word of coin. In that way, there is no problem when persons continue to use the word "mode" inappropriately, because it is no longer confused with the word "modal." Dorian, Phrygian, Lydian, Mixolydian, Aeolian, and Locrian are both modes and modal, but major and minor are only modes. The word "tonality" includes all modes as well as major and minor. In current usage, tonality is associated with modes, rather than keys. That is a compelling, or might I say convincing, resolution.

Carl, if you were to revise your test, would you be disposed to consider the evolved concept of tonality?

Seashore I don't think so. Then, even the thought of key was anathema to me. It was clear to implicate key modulations in a test of music aptitude would transform the test into one of music achievement. Further, involving tonality would have had even more deleterious effects.

Suzuki So, Lowell, you are saying there are seven tonalities, five of which are modal and two are not. What about key, and atonal music? Are they anomalies?

Mason I will get to those presently. For now, mode has superseded key in importance in the thinking, if not audiation, of a minority of contemporary music psychologists, educators, theorists, and performing musicians of many stripes, colors, and dots.

Suzuki You're not saying the word "key" has outlived its usefulness, are you?

Mason In a way, yes, but please remember, I am the messenger, not the message.

I find it amazing there were, and still are, music theorists, editors, and practitioners who teach if any kind of pentatonic song ends, for example, on "re," it is in Dorian tonality. They don't understand without harmonic accompaniment to indirectly suggest otherwise, it is not possible to identify objectively the tonality of a song unless it includes characteristic pitches. For example, in Dorian, the characteristic pitches are "do" and "ti," the subtonic and raised sixth, respectively. Without inclusion of the raised sixth, "ti," the resting tone, "re," could just as well be audiated as "la," thus suggesting Aeolian tonality.

That reasoning may, of course, be logically generalized to all tonalities. Although a major sounding song may end on "so," without a lowered seventh, "fa," being sounded to indicate Mixolydian tonality, "so" might just as well be audiated as "do," the resting tone of major tonality.

Jaques-Dalcroze I gather your explanation is in terms of movable "do" with a "la" based minor.

Mason Of course. I hope by now I have shown the value and simplicity of movable "do" with a "la" based minor. Neither music theory, notation, or use of chromatic syllables is necessary to elucidate intrinsic musical concepts, such as tonality, when using that system. All that is required is to audiate the resting tone and bestow upon it the only possible one of seven syllable names.

Yes Èmile, I know, chromatic syllables are not used with the immovable "do" system, but I would not like to be appointed teacher if I had to instruct musical neophytes to sing different pitches using the same syllable. I believe that anomaly, a glitch, you know, was mentioned heretofore. By the way Èmile, one's perfect pitch would give rise to only a letter name, perhaps a key, but not a tonality.

Orff What about use of numbers?

Mason As far as I can tell, they might have use for explaining the theory of an ascending major scale, but I can think of no other advantage.

Orff Numbers are familiar.

Seashore That is so, but it is for that very reason numbers have limited practicality. It is difficult to learn to transfer the same technique from one use to another. Familiar use of numbers blocks learning an unfamiliar one. Psychologists refer to that as retroactive inhibition. Asking children to skip numbers and count backward is an intellectual exploit, not easily accomplished by most, particularly when they are accustomed to using numbers in ordinal and cardinal fashions. They have learned to count beginning with one.

Kodály Are you, Lowell, going to continue and discuss key and keyality or will Carl Seashore?

Seashore I know I don't measure up to any of you in musicianship. Let me try to explain to see if I truly understand the concepts myself.

Mason Carry on, Carl.

Seashore Consider the note "A." It has two meanings: a specific sound in terms of the frequency, 440, and it is a place on a staff. It does not indicate a key? Now think of three sharps. Does that indicate a key. No, not anymore than a letter name does. Both are only keys to where "do" is found on the staff. Note names, or sharps or flats, or the absence of signs altogether, simply identify a line or space on the staff.

Kodály What is traditionally called a key signature is actually a "do" signature. Carl's explanation is accurate; however, the key of a piece of music is not revealed until tonality is established in audiation. For example, imagine a staff with one sharp at the beginning. Some marginally informed persons may say the music is in the key of "G." But, one sharp may indicate the key of "E" if the music is in minor tonality; "A" if in Dorian tonality;" "B" if in Phrygian tonality; "C" if in Lydian tonality; "D" if in Mixolydian tonality; and "F#" if Locrian tonality.

Seashore Fascinating! Just as, for example, "A" minor is relative to "C" major, also "D" Dorian is relative to "C" major; "E" Phrygian to "C" major; "F" Lydian to "C" major; "G" Mixolydian to "C" major; and "B" Locrian to "C" major.

Kodály So, the word "key" must be understood in its practical meaning. It is simply and only a key to the location of "do" on a staff. It does not indicate a keyality.

Jaques-Dalcroze Keyality, I gather is a current word.

Kodály Well, we can disperse with the word "key' and substitute it with the word "keyality" and use the term "'do' signature." What is usually called a key signature might best be called a "do" signature.

Seashore What else about keyality?

Kodály You see a "do" signature, it is visible, whereas you audiate a keyality. It is as straightforward and uncomplicated as that.

Jaques-Dalcroze Is a "do" signature still relevant if music is in a tonality other than major?

Kodály Yes. Suppose you see a "do" signature of two flats and music is being audiated in minor tonality. It is quickly generalized that because "do" is, for example, on the third line of the treble staff, "la," being audiated as the resting tone, is on the line below, and therefore, the music is in G keyality. If the music were in Dorian tonality, the keyality would be C with "re" being audiated as the resting tone on the third space, the space above the third line. The same is true for all tonalities. The Guidonian hand is most useful in teaching this concept.

Seashore Let me put that in my own words. Teaching students to memorize an abundance of so-called key signatures is emblematic of an exercise in musical crossword puzzles. Such activity, associated with music theory, is an example of the difference between having something to teach and having to teach something. It is no wonder so many students are frightened and driven away from the study of music.

Corybant Unnecessary theoretical balderdash.

Jaques-Dalcroze Here I am as the gadfly again. I would like to hear about how all this accommodates atonality.

Suzuki May I respond? If I am myopic, please set me straight. I recently stumbled upon some contemporary writing that has me philosophizing, be it right or wrong, in this way. I'm curious about what you all think.

Music commonly referred to as atonal is in fact multitonal. The word "multitonal" seems preferable because so-called atonal music is not without tonality. Extensive multitonal music includes many rapidly changing tonalities, usually in association with many rapidly changing keyalities. Thus, music probably sounds atonal only to persons who cannot audiate rapidly changing tonalities and keyalities. That atonal has been misunderstood and misused is attested to even by Arnold Schoenberg, the composer credited with having developed the twelve-tone system.

I will quote Schoenberg. "I resent your statements about 'atonalism,' a term which I never used." More relevant are two thoughts found in Bruckner-Mahler-Schoenberg by Dika Newlin: "Schoenberg, I am well aware, abhorred this word—atonal—because of its negative connotations. However, since his preferred term 'pantonality' never gained wide currency in the sense in which he used it, I have used the more commonly understood 'atonality.' ... Tonality and atonality are not mutually exclusive."

Corybant I would like to add something. Music can be multikeyal as well as multitonal. Multikeyal music includes at least two, though usually more, objective and/or subjective keyalities.

Jaques-Dalcroze Is that the extent of it?

Mason I've heard it said there is no atonal music, only a-audiational listeners.

Suzuki Just a bit more. Some music theorists are actually convinced they can initiate a new method using intervals to read notation. They judge relative size of contiguous horizontal intervals is the basis for tonal organization. However, to perceive the size of an interval, rather than audiating its function in a tonal context, is suspect. Meanwhile, other music theorists posit, for purposes of dealing with what they call atonal music, that it is beneficial to associate interval names verbally with sounds without reference to the tonality in which the intervals are found.

Corybant On the basis of previous discussions, I had intended to suggest we compare music theory and audiation. At this point, perhaps anything more to be said would be superfluous, if not redundant.

I have not forgotten your curiosity about present-day music learning and how it relates to common practice music theory. When shall we engage in that discussion?

Mason I suggest another rest period and time to think. May we decide our direction upon our return. There are so many interesting topics that could be profitably introduced. For example, can emotion in music be explained in terms of practical language? If so, would that have value for teaching music?

Kodály Lowell, I too, have several questions.

Corybant And let's leave it at that. I think it inevitable, however, that we will soon dedicate as much thought to rhythm as we have to its tonal counterpart.

X: Rhythm Essentials

von Laban I am becoming impatient. We have addressed movement, dance, rhythm patterns, rhythm solfege, breathing, and coordination at length, but Èmile and I think the group has unintentionally sidestepped rhythm itself.

Carl Orff, is rhythm fundamental to music?

Orff It is seminal.

von Laban Hector Berlioz said, "Such is the tremendous field of rhythm that who cultivates it will harvest riches."

Jaques-Dalcroze Agreed.

von Laban Zoltán is an esteemed linguist. Talk to us, Zoltán, about the etymology of the word "rhythm."

Kodály "Rhythm" comes from Greek *rhythmos*. It means flow, as water in a river. In Latin, *mov* means movement and *mot* means motion. The Latin infinitive *movere* means to move. Rhythm, and possibly emotion, were associated with movement in the minds of early thinkers.

von Laban Carl Orff, what about attempts to clarify the nature of rhythm?

Orff Most traditional explanations of rhythm in music, even when based on the relation of meter to early metrical structure of poetry disregard movement. They explain rhythm in terms of accents, fractions, and counting. Some even usurp pulse and tempo.

Corybant To comprehend the intrinsic properties of rhythm, musicians now make distinctions among different types of beats, meters, and between meter and tempo. If I seem to harbor some misunderstanding, you must assist me. Although I have participated musically in worship rites, I am not, nor do I pretend to be, an educated musician.

What I think is capturing minds of music educators is on the cusp of coming change. Remember, I am just repeating what I have heard and read, particularly in Learning Sequences in Music: A Contemporary Music Learning Theory.

von Laban Is this a recent book?

Corybant Yes, it is a 2007 revision, perhaps the seventh, published by GIA in Chicago, Illinois, in the United States of America. There are marked changes from one progressive version to the next. I hope my summary is sufficient.

In both usual and unusual meters, three elements define rhythm: macrobeats, microbeats, and rhythm patterns. We have spoken of these words and terms when discussing movement. Macrobeats are fundamental to feeling microbeats and rhythm patterns, because microbeats and rhythm patterns are superimposed on macrobeats in audiation. Microbeats are shorter than macrobeats and are derived from the equal division of macrobeats.

When macrobeats are divided into two microbeats of equal length, the first of two coinciding with a macrobeat, the result is usual duple meter. When macrobeats are divided into three microbeats of equal length, the first of three coinciding with a macrobeat, the result is usual triple meter. When some macrobeats are divided into two microbeats of equal length and other macrobeats are divided into three microbeats of equal length, regardless of sequence of groupings, the result is usual combined meter. In usual combined meter, all macrobeats are of equal length, but not all microbeats are of equal length.

Music is considered to be in usual meter only when macrobeats are audiated in pairs and are of equal length. When audiated together, macrobeats, microbeats, and rhythm patterns lose individual qualities and uniquely interact as a whole. All three symbiotically become one, that is, rhythm.

Jaques-Dalcroze What is unusual meter?

Corybant When macrobeats are not of equal length, music is in unusual meter. This is so whether or not one audiates macrobeats in pairs, regardless of their sequence. However, microbeats are of equal length in unusual meter. Some macrobeats may include two microbeats, others three microbeats, and some may not be divided at all. That is, macrobeats may be intact.

There are four types of unusual meter: unusual paired, unusual unpaired, unusual paired intact, and unusual unpaired intact. The basic distinction between usual meter and unusual meter is that in usual meter, the issue is how macrobeats of equal length are divided. In unusual meter, the concern is how macrobeats of unequal lengths are grouped. In usual meter, microbeats establish meter and macrobeats establish tempo. In unusual meter, it is the opposite. Macrobeats establish meter and microbeats establish tempo.

Jaques-Dalcroze What is intact meter?

Corybant In unusual intact meter, some macrobeats are the length of three microbeats, some the length of two microbeats, and others the length of only one microbeat. A macrobeat the length of only one microbeat is called an intact macrobeat, because the two types of beats occur simultaneously. An intact macrobeat is found only in unusual meter. Because an intact macrobeat is heard simultaneously with itself as its only microbeat, the two are concurrent in audiation and performance.

Intact macrobeats can be divided into only divisions of microbeats, and they are always found in combination with other longer macrobeats in a rhythm pattern that are divided into microbeats of twos and threes or into only twos or only threes. In a rhythm pattern, a macrobeat may be paired with any other macrobeat, including another intact macrobeat, or it may be unpaired. In audiation, the listener subjectively decides which macrobeats are paired and unpaired.

von Laban Thank you. The ideas are imaginative and thought provoking. As you were speaking, Corybant, I could not help but think about time signatures and how they came into being.

Corybant I can relay some information about that, too. Introductory statements, however, which I believe are necessary, will be almost as long as the pith. I will need your extended forbearance.

In the seventeenth and eighteenth centuries, rhythm notation, as we know it today, began to emerge. Note values, measure signatures, and measure lines were used. However, only mensural signs of common time and cut time survived.

Suzuki Mensural?

Orff Yes. When each note has a definite and exact time value. This relates to polyphonic music, which originated in the 13th century.

Suzuki Thank you.

Corybant How the transition from mensural notation, the old signs, to current notational practice, the new signs, took place between approximately 1650 to 1800 remains unclear. As usual, facts have been forced to fit theories in attempts to explain and interpret rhythm notation.

Going back, now, to Professor Riemann, the terms "simple duple," "compound duple," "simple triple," and "compound triple" are often defined in relation to measure signatures. The same terms are also used to explain meter. As you know, students are taught meter in music is determined by the number of beats in a measure, indicated by measure signatures. How macrobeats are divided and grouped is ignored.

For example, students learn music in 2/4 is simple duple meter; duple because there are two beats—quarter notes—in a measure and simple because each beat is divided into two beats—eighth notes. They are taught only twos need be considered. There is no attempt to distinguish between types of beats.

Likewise, students learn music in 6/8 is compound duple meter; duple because there are two beats—dotted quarter notes—in a measure and compound because each beat is divided into three beats—eighth notes. Both twos and threes need to be considered.

Duple and triple can be audiated and demonstrated in movement, but simple and compound cannot, because their meanings hinge entirely on arithmetic associated with the notation of measure signatures. Astonishing! The words "simple" and "compound" continue to be used with abandon in an attempt to define meter, rhythm notwithstanding.

Orff I think all that is our common concern.

Corybant Good.

Further, students are taught music in 3/4 is simple triple meter; triple, because there are three beats—quarter notes—in a measure and simple because each beat is divided into two beats—eighth notes. Even though both twos and threes need to be considered, this is called simple. The inconsistency partially results from the mistaken belief note values indicate whether a note functions as a macrobeat or a microbeat. However, note values do not indicate types of beats.

For example, typically a quarter note is a macrobeat and an eighth note a microbeat in 2/4. A dotted quarter note is a macrobeat and an eighth note a microbeat in 6/8. A dotted whole note is a macrobeat and a half note a microbeat in 6/4.

When macrobeats are audiated in terms of weight rather than accents, meter underlying two measures of 3/4 is audiated in the same manner as meter underlying one measure of 6/8.

Mason I assume, then, a dotted half note in 3/4 is equal to a dotted quarter note in 6/8.

Corybant Yes. Both are usual triple meter. For example, consider *Silent Night*. Unless you were apprised of the notation of the song, you would not be sure whether what is being performed is notated using 3/4 or 6/8. Just as two key signatures can be enharmonic, so two measure signatures, such as 3/4 compared with 6/8, and 2/4 compared with 4/4 and 2/8, can be enrhythmic. Not intending to monopolize the discussion…

von Laban I'm interested. Please go on.

Corybant Music written in 9/8 is commonly taught as being compound triple meter; triple because there are three beats—dotted quarter notes—in a measure and compound because each beat is divided into three beats—eighth notes. It is called compound even though only threes need to be considered, but again, that inconsistency is routinely overlooked.

von Laban Does this mean 1/4 should be called simple single?

Corybant Well said, clever fellow! Considerations about simple versus compound aside, it is important to observe in 9/8 three dotted quarter notes together equal one macrobeat. A dotted quarter note represents a microbeat, not a macrobeat, and eighth notes represent divisions of a microbeat. One measure of nine eighth notes in 9/8 is audiated as if it were written as one measure of 3/4 using three eighth note triplets, or as half a measure of 6/8 written using three sixteenth note triplets. All three measure signatures—9/8, 3/4, and 6/8—may be, and usually are, enrhythmic. Every one typically represents usual triple meter.

Those who rely on notation instead of audiation to interpret music notation may incorrectly decide music in 3/4 or 9/8 represents unusual unpaired meter. They believe in both cases there are three macrobeats in a measure, with one macrobeat going unpaired. If macrobeats in a rhythm pattern are of equal length, they cannot represent unusual meter. Theory-bound persons fail to understand what they believe is notated as macrobeats are actually audiated as microbeats.

von Laban Enrhythmic, right?

Corybant Yes. Rhythm patterns that sound the same but are notated differently, and different measure signatures used to notate the same meter. That's what enrhythmic means. Enrhythmic is to durations and measure signatures what enharmonic is to pitches and key signatures.

von Laban I like that.

Corybant Examining conventional explanations is critical to understanding rhythm and meter. Although much may seem new, everything is firmly grounded in the past.

Relevant and instructive references are in Robert Donington's, The Interpretation of Early Music. In Bourdelot-Bonnet's Historie de la Musique (Paris, 1725), Le Cerf de La Vieville says "So there are in general only two measures, that in two-time and that in three; in vain would you wish to imagine others." And Charles Masson wrote in his Nouveau Traite, Paris, 1701, "Although there appear to be a quantity of different measures, I believe that it is useful to point out that there is only the number two or three which divides them." In Elements or Principles of Music, published in the 17th century, Étienne Loulié says the following about duple compound meter written with the measure signature 6/16. "Since this meter is composed of two triple meters, students can conduct each in three beats, making two measures out of one."

Measures written to include two underlying macrobeats were originally called compound, and so it seems distinctions made between simple and compound were derived from notation, not audiation of meter. Regrettably, traditional definitions of meter make no provision for discriminating between usual meter and unusual meter, or among different meters. Two additional books offer rich information: Nikolaus Harnoncourt's Baroque Music Today: Music as Speech. Ways to a New Understanding of Music and George Houle's Meter in Music, 1600-1800. Performance, Perception, and Notation.

Jaques-Dalcroze Corybant, would you please summarize the salient points of measure signatures? I have always referred to them as time or meter signatures.

Corybant As explained in the literature, a measure signature is not a meter signature, because it does not indicate any specific meter. Nor is it a time signature, because it does not indicate a specific time or tempo. The same meter may be notated using different measure signatures and the same measure signature may be used to notate different meters. That measure signatures can serve enrhythmically in notation attests to the fact meter of a piece of music is most appropriately determined through body movement and audiation, not by memorizing inadequate and misleading definitions. Historically, meter was determined through dance and audiation. Notation and theoretical definitions caused modern-day confusion.

von Laban Yes, yes, yes! All rhythm is movement. Movement internalized in the body, in terms of feeling space and time, becomes eternal rhythm. To control movement is to develop rhythmic mentality. Oh, if only children remained children and resisted adult indoctrination. Movements of small children are beautiful, purely physical and unconscious. That is the way musicians should reveal rhythm. Instrumentalists and vocalists could learn so much by participating in dance choirs. Sorry to interrupt you, Corybant.

Corybant Numerals in a measure signature refer to macrobeats or microbeats, not simply to beats. For example, numerals in a measure signature used to notate usual duple meter usually relate to macrobeats, as in 2/4, where 2 indicates two macrobeats in a measure and 4 indicates a quarter note represents a macrobeat.

However, numerals in a measure signature used to notate usual triple meter usually relate to microbeats, as in 6/8, where 6 indicates six microbeats in a measure and 8 indicates an eighth note represents a microbeat. The dotted quarter note represents a macrobeat.

Numerals in a measure signature used to notate unusual meters usually relate to microbeats. In 5/8, for example, 5 indicates five microbeats in a measure and 8 indicates an eighth note represents a microbeat. The quarter and dotted quarter notes represent the two macrobeats in a measure. Of course, an eighth note may also indicate an intact macrobeat. When 2/4 is used to notate unusual paired intact meter or unusual unpaired intact meter, numerals in a measure signature do not automatically represent either macrobeats or microbeats.

Jaques-Dalcroze I cannot say I absorbed all that, but primary and secondary accents, in contrast to atonicity, remain pivotal in my understanding of what I still consider a meter signature. I insist there is a difference between 2/4 and 4/4, and between 3/4 and 6/8.

Dalcrozian concepts of meter and rhythm are an integral part of music theory and aural skills classes in some institutions of higher education. With regard to meter signatures, the three foremost components in Dalcroze teaching are solfege, which teaches inner hearing; improvisation; and Eurhythmics. Eurhythmics is the last to be developed.

Mason Perhaps in theory dynamic accents prevail, but certainly rarely, if ever, in audiation, and only for special effects in artistic performance. Agogic accents, on the other hand, are another matter.

von Laban Movement must be emphasized whenever the topic of rhythm is raised, if rhythm is to be comprehended realistically.

In analyzing movement arts and visual arts, I discovered I did not need to rely on music or mime to structure dance. One of my goals was to free the body by mirroring it in movement and dance. Sigmund Freud opened the door and freed me to display the body's sexual needs, no longer hidden to please or mollify pseudo-sophisticated audiences. In the interplay between body, mind, and psyche, I gave special attention to learning to imitate specific body parts, connecting them to one another, and then sequencing their movement.

Mason Rudolf, a moment ago you spoke of importance of dance choirs. That brought to mind something that should not be overlooked. It is common knowledge most students and musicians achieve at higher levels tonally than rhythmically. I believe I know the main reason for this incongruity. Most students take private lessons when learning to play a music instrument. When playing solo, they adhere to their own rhythm, which often deviates from accuracy. If they were taught in ensembles, they would listen to one another and thus, become cognizant of contextual rhythm. Not only would their rhythm be more accurate, their sense of stabilized tempo would be solidified. Furthermore, tempo rubato would then likely assume its important place in musical expression.

Suzuki That should give students and teachers of piano and organ pause for concern.

Kodály Group lessons, both instrumental and vocal, would undoubtedly improve intonation as well as rhythm.

von Laban Corybant has recommended books that may be consulted. In the sense of being a tribune, I would like to add two recent books to the directory. The first was written by a physiotherapist: Irmgard Bartenieff. The title is Fundamentals. Understand, it is not simply because the author is knowledgeable of my work that I herald and advocate it highly. The other book, The Elusive Obvious, was authored by Moshe Feldenkrais.

I've said enough. A mind exposed to a new idea can never regain its original shape. Solitude is necessary for that process to unfold.

Corybant Any humor?

Seashore I've heard it said theoreticians use a measure signature for the same purpose an inebriated person uses a lamppost: for support rather than illumination.

Corybant Sarcasm, the lowest form of humor.

I nearly forgot. One more important thought before we disperse: Just as there is multitonal and multikeyal music, so there is multimetric and multitemporal music. With regard to these two tonal elements, tonality and keyality are audiated subjectively. Likewise, with regard to these two rhythm elements, meter and tempo are audiated subjectively. And with that, I say rest well, without limitary thoughts, and return with exuberance to partake in and be challenged by what is to come.

XI: Instrumental Music

Suzuki Corybant, we have directed the majority of our time to discussions about classroom music. I have found it interesting, but I would like to talk about instrumental music. Carl Orff and I agree it would be a timely topic.

    Carl is focused on primitive and mallet instruments designed to be used in classroom creativity and improvisation. I am interested in more traditional instrumental music pedagogy. I'm sure you know my passion is violin, but I have taught students to perform on other instruments as well. May we now turn to teaching students to perform using string, brass, woodwind, and percussion instruments? Later, I feel sure, Carl will contribute comments about mallet instruments and their role in guiding improvisation and creativity in the classroom.

Jaques-Dalcroze You know, Shinicki, in my Eurhythmic classes, every student memorized an instrumental part of a familiar or unfamiliar composition and then sang it with and without accompanied body movement, in class as an ensemble.

Corybant Anything goes, as long as the topic is stimulating.

von Laban You know me as a dancer and movement coach. I danced in the Moulin Rouge and toured in North Africa in a review. Later I danced in Leipzig, Dresden, and Münster, Germany, and in Vienna, Austria.

Jaques-Dalcroze I spent time in Algiers, much of my time performing as a dinner pianist. I found Africa as intoxicating as you did.

von Laban My father was a field marshal, a general if you will, in the army of the Austro-Hungarian Empire. He planned a military career for me, but fate intervened. As a result of my parents constantly traveling, they decided I should be reared by an aunt and uncle in Bosnia and Herzegovina. With their permission, I abandoned my father's vocational path and was allowed to partake in artistic endeavors.

  I married twice and fathered nine children, but never was thought of as a family man. I courted poor health and was insolvent all my life. Others assumed I was depressed. I was diagnosed by a doctor as being manic depressive. Well, of course! Actors with whom I worked, however, held an entirely different opinion of me. Fortunately, they, dancers, musicians, and physical and psycho therapists, not to mention apprentices, carried on my ideas as I concentrated on one and then impatiently and eagerly moved to another.

Seashore Interesting. Déjà vu.

von Laban And I want you to know how I love opera, particular Wagner's later creations. When I was a ballet director at the Berlin State Opera and Kroll Opera, I realized there are three types of dance: festive, theatre, and independent art. It was the internal disposition of humans, not external influences of environment, that conquered my zeal. As a result, I composed opera-ballets and dance dramas. I discovered three types of rhythm. The rhythm of ornaments affects our seeing, the rhythm of music affects our hearing, and the rhythm of movement affects out vitality.

  Now that you are sentient about my involvement with opera, it should be clear why I think it no less important than other milieus we have entertained. But that is not to imply I think we should not talk about instrumental music teaching. We must, but can we reserve some time for opera? I ask this while being cognizant of what Zoltán has said about Magyar music: "A music teacher in Kisvárda is more important then the director of opera in Budapest."

XI: Instrumental Music

Corybant I have been making ongoing notes. Without making any promises, I shall add opera to my list of potential topics to be introduced. Of course. I suspect time, however, will make decisions for us.

Shinicki, would you please initiate the topic of instrumental music teaching and your unique revolutionary method, or was it a matter of evolution?

von Laban But…

Corybant I promise, Rudolf.

Suzuki Thank you, Rudolf, for that sketch of your background. You've inspired me to mention a few words about myself. Though history has pigeonholed me, I have engaged in more than violin pedagogy. My three honorary doctorates notwithstanding, in 1928 I was a concert violinist. Before that, I assisted my father as a violin maker in his factory while studying the design of string instruments.

von Laban Tame, but interesting.

Suzuki When Pau, you know him as Pablo Casals, said music will save the world, there was not a scintilla of doubt in my mind. He was correct. I have devoted my life to substantiating that empowering conviction. I began with faith music could help rejuvenate young Japanese children devastated by World War II. All this is why I call my pedagogy education instead of instruction. I constantly keep in mind three important educational goals: musical sense, performance ability, and character in the mind.

My father was an educated man who taught English. He taught me the word "education" is a derivative of "educe," meaning to draw or bring out. Drawing knowledge from a student is in stark disparity with typical instruction, in which a teacher attempts to push what he or she knows into a student. In my opinion, that is ill-advised.

When I first began my career as a violin teacher, I was shocked to discover the great majority of my students had been taught to perform mechanically. They were becoming forced musicians, and I use the word "musicians" gratuitously. Their instrumental technique was emphasized with little, if any, conscious concern for musicality. Although they made sense of music notation and could transfer to their instrument what symbols indicate, they lacked adequate understanding of what symbols represent in sound.

Strictly speaking, a symbol represents something. Notes in music notation are symbols intended to represent musical sounds, not simply directions for placing fingers on a fingerboard. My students were not audiating. They could not sing what music notation indicated until they called upon their instruments to interpret it. Even then, the outcome was dubious.

Jaques-Dalcroze I, too, am becoming attracted to the word "audiation," but not smitten with it. I maintain allegiance to my own term "inner hearing." I really don't see a difference between audiation and inner hearing.

Kodály One can inner hear something but not understand it. For example, say "ag ga da." Now, can you inner hear it? Can you say it to yourself silently? Of course you can. Now tell me what it means. You can't. You are inner hearing but not audiating. If you knew what it meant, you would be audiating, not just inner hearing. With regard to language, we think, not audiate.

Mason I have had choir members who could memorize a piece of music perfectly, but if I stopped in the middle of a piece and asked anyone to sing the tonal center, the resting tone, only a minority could. They were inner hearing, I suspect, without audiating. It would have been pointless to ask them whether the music was in major or minor, or duple or triple.

Seashore Perhaps they memorized what they were hearing internally.

Suzuki I would not dispute that.

Kodály I empathetically understand what Shinicki has said. When I was teaching at the Liszt Academy in Budapest, Hungary, I allowed students to enter my studio as I was completing the final few minutes of a piano lesson with the student who preceded them. Imagine! More than one student was totally unaware that he or she was learning the same composition the other student was playing. But, I must say, they could execute the same notes at the keyboard without hesitation. I was astonished and wondered whether I was wasting my or students' time. That experience catapulted me into music education of the young.

That being said, Émile, I will continue to use your term, "inner hearing," but with new understanding. As we grow in age it becomes more difficult for us to change.

Corybant Contumacy, no! It doesn't matter how old you are. Change can instill fear in all of us. Even transition from fear to ambivalence requires effort.

Suzuki Speaking of age, using instruments of various sizes, I accepted students as young as three, and with due respect to Carl Seashore and his followers, I had no entrance test. I knew a good environment would bring out superior talent in all children, regardless of natural endowment.

Seashore You say you taught to students' individual differences. What criteria did you use? How did you identify their individual musical needs?

Suzuki Simply by watching and listening to their playing, and keeping track of the quality of their environment. Parents were indispensable in that regard.

Seashore So, you adapted instruction on the basis of music achievement and attitude. Is that so?

Suzuki I know you will insist those criteria are subjective, but they worked. Experience is my advocate.

Seashore Did you ever compare the validity of your subjective analyses to results on an objective measure, such as a valid music aptitude test?

Suzuki No, the opportunity did not present itself. Even if it did, I'm not sure I would have administered a music aptitude test.

Seashore How about a valid music achievement test?

Suzuki I probably would not have administered that either. I trusted my experiential judgment. For example, if students could talk while playing accurately, that confirmed they had acquired a given level of technical skill. A good teacher is the main ingredient for success.

My pedagogical reasoning was uncomplicated. Using how children learn language, I developed what I call the mother tongue method. Children listened to music as an introductory step to playing in the same manner that they listened to their native language for approximately a year before they began to speak. They listened to one recording played over and over again, and then another in the same manner. In music, speaking is singing and performing instrumentally.

I emphasize, singing must be a requisite for playing a music instrument. How else will one know how to play in tune?

Jaques-Dalcroze Shinicki, please don't slight listening. The sequence might best be described as listening, singing, and playing an instrument.

Suzuki I thought I made that clear.

Kodály I agree. Learning to play a music instrument should come after a student has developed listening and vocal skills.

von Laban Don't forget movement and proper breathing. I would argue they come early on.

Suzuki Good intonation results from adjusting what is being produced on a music instrument to what is being audiated, or as others might prefer, inner heard. Thanks to vibrato, there is ample time to make physical pitch adjustments. I think a contemporary performer said, vibrato is to musicians what molding is to carpenters: Both cover a multitude of sins.

Mason Perfection is a wonderful goal, but without realization it is unobtainable, possibilities are precluded.

Corybant You will not believe what I just read in a recent, 21st century, tabloid. Admonitions offered by music educators were that parents must be sure their children can count and recite the alphabet before being given lessons on a music instrument. In that way, the children will develop self-discipline, concentration, memory, and motor skills. What is there to say to uninformed teachers who foster displaced musical readiness?

Mason A nettling problem.
  But what about this? There are educationalists who base their pedagogy on learning styles. They claim some students learn better, for example, by listening than seeing and therefore, instruction should be adapted to their proclivity. If students in a music class are visual rather than aural learners, it is recommended their attention be directed to spelling words on a staff rather than listening to music. How does one explain the inanity of evoking that alternative?

Jaques-Dalcroze Suggest to the teacher that students in an art class who are aural learners put paint brushes in their ears.

Corybant Carry on, Shinicki.

Suzuki My procedure was from rote to note, using memorized finger patterns. The sequence was listening, performing vocally and instrumentally, and reading. Technical mastery preceded reading. Vibrato, trilling, and expression were accentuated. I was careful not to choose music that might be too difficult to learn so students would not be inclined to discontinue lessons.

Parents assumed a vital role. *Twinkle, Twinkle, Little Star* became a core. I found advanced students' private lessons with parents in attendance to be most rewarding. I expected parents to supervise their child's home practice. Although all students followed the same pedagogical sequence, they participated in group festivals according to their individual levels of development. All stood while playing, and they were not exposed to any paraphernalia. Nevertheless, playing was fun.

Seashore If all students are born with the same natural ability, how did you account for different levels of achievement among groups you taught?

Suzuki Carl, that's obvious. They began studying at different times and ages.

Seashore Don't you think natural endowment might have had even a small role in their achievement?

Suzuki I doubt it. Practice and study procedures are determining factors. When students learn one section of a piece by playing it many times before moving to the next, the end result is realized.

Orff Interesting. When on earth, I came across research results declaring overlearning was not only unproductive, it many cases it was detrimental.

Suzuki What is overlearning?

Orff Say it takes one hour to learn an étude. If you keep practicing it for an additional hour, that is 100% overlearning. If, instead, you keep practicing it for another half hour, that is 50% overlearning, and so on.

XI: Instrumental Music

Suzuki Well, call it what you will, it worked for me and my students.

Mason It seems to me, Shinicki, you depended a great deal on imitation and memorization.

Suzuki That's true. I acknowledge that.

Mason Do you see an association between imitation and audiation, and a dissociation between memorization and audiation?

Suzuki All this is new to me. I need time to think it through. Why not ask Èmile? His curriculum stressed scales and melodic dictation. Students even named notes associated with workaday sounds.

Jaques-Dalcroze I, too, need time to think. Truly, I need to hear more discussion.

Corybant That's why were are here.

Mason It seems Carl Orff read widely during his earthly life, whereas I have read much more after my arrival in the firmament. What I have absorbed is this: current thought is students learn two instruments, the audiation instrument and the actual music instrument. To make satisfactory progress, they should practice their audiation instrument as preparation for learning to play the actual music instrument

Suzuki I agree. I think I have been saying the same thing using different words. Doesn't listening give rise to audiation?

Mason That, along with other ideas, sanctions dubious popular opinion. For example, traditionally, a child's physical characteristics determine the instrument for which he or she is best suited. Some bass players are taught the instrument because they are tall. Violinists start on the instrument because they have long fingers or small hands. Although a child's motor dexterity should be a consideration, there appears to be little evidence, either empirically or experimentally, to suggest physical factors are of much consequence.

In fact, many professional instrumentalists' physical characteristics gainsay conventional beliefs about who should play what. However, evidence does suggest although initially elementary school students may be attracted to a music instrument because of its appearance or other irrelevant reasons, in time they will enjoy most success when they study a music instrument with tone quality and range that appeals to them.

Corybant Go on.

Mason What I find mesmerizing is two sets of research findings. First, it appears unnecessary to spend much time teaching formation of an embouchure on a wind instrument or when to raise and lower fingers on a fingerboard of a string instrument to students who audiate tonally. They naturally develop an internal pitch selector to produce the pitch they are audiating. Meanwhile, if students audiate exemplary tone quality before they produce physical sound, they will learn, one way or another, to produce that tone quality on their instrument. Characteristically, young students have no idea of the sound they are expected to produce. Unless they audiate a preferred tone quality, it is reasonable to believe they cannot be expected to produce it.

Second, deficiency in ability in what is referred to as sight reading music notation is really a lack of audiation skill, not necessarily a lack of cognitive or instrumental skill. If students cannot read with fluency even though they can decode notes, they are not reading musically because they cannot audiate what the sound of the notes, the symbols, represent. Simply put, if students can't read notation of familiar music, of course they can't sight read. Sight reading is nothing more than reading unfamiliar music notation. Reading is reading, whether music notation or music itself is familiar or unfamiliar. When a student cannot sight read, it follows the student actually has not been taught to read.

It seems the term "sight reading" shadows the fact that many teachers, for whatever the reason, disregard their responsibility for appropriately teaching the reading of music notation. Music theory has superseded music praxis.

Seashore Isn't all reading accomplished through sight? As you said, reading is reading, and sight is the vehicle to accomplish the mission. I never heard of anyone smell reading.

Corybant Most, if not all, of you have expressed more need for thoughtful solitude. Include me in that band. So, let's take an unusually long break, but remember, regrettably, time is not unlimited. Soon you all will be going your separate ways. I'll be waiting here to greet you when we assemble again. You might decide upon your return if you desire to re-examine topics or introduce new ones. There is so much that might be considered. Don't forget opera.

Everyone seems so serious.

Jaques-Dalcroze I have a question. What's the difference between a contemporary pop musician and a jazz musician?

A contemporary pop musician plays three chords for a thousand listeners. A jazz musician plays a thousand chords for three listeners.

von Laban I have a definition of minimalism. It's a style of composition in which an orchestra vamps until ready, but no one is ever ready.

Corybant It is time to bid a temporary farewell. Rest well, and delight in the elixir energy of diversity.

XII: Patterns

Kodály Rest well we did, and here we are again. I propose we begin with a discussion of patterns. We have mentioned patterns hither and thither, but have not fully analyzed their significance in relation to individual pitches and durations. Èmile, are patterns taught in Eurhythmics? I recall, you, Carl Orff, gave some consideration to patterns.

Jaques-Dalcroze When students move around the room, they must be aware of patterns.

Kodály Perhaps rhythm patterns, but what about tonal patterns? Carl, what say you?

Orff I suspect dancing involves rhythm patterns, but, Èmile, you and I are not on the same wavelength.

Jaques-Dalcroze Zoltán, explain what you mean.

Kodály Certainly, but a little introductory background first. As a nationalist, I wanted to restore Hungarian folk music to its rightful place in the country's culture but also, it was my goal to educate the populace successfully and thus, bring music into the home. More recently, György Ligeti followed the same path. I, like most of you, encountered cretins as well as mavens in my quest, the former, though not their fault, being in the majority. They had a poor music education. I came to the conclusion they were inundated with too much theory and not enough practice. I then had to identify appropriate practice. My colleagues and I watched and listened in primary school classrooms in various cities. I settled on the belief students could benefit much more from listening to and performing patterns of music than by concentrating on theoretical intricacies of individual notes.

The wellspring is this: tonal patterns and rhythm patterns are fundamental in understanding music. Individual pitches and durations simply advance linearly to and fro in flow of melody. In contrast, tonal patterns move in irregular linear space toward and away from one or more tonal centers, and rhythm patterns move in continuous circular space as they relate to number and grouping of underlying beats. Thus, patterns, not isolated sounds, are compelling fonts of what we, in our group, call content within context in music. I had to discover a way to convey this concept to music teachers so they could pass it on to students. In Kodály methodology, tonal patterns and rhythm patterns claim essential roles.

Orff Was this concept original with you?

Kodály An American contemporary also recognized importance of patterns. John W. Beattie, who lived from 1885 to 1962, was a professor and an administrator at Northwestern University in Evanston, Illinois. He was also an editor of The American Singer. The series was designed for students in classroom music instruction. At the top of every song on a page was a tonal pattern. The songs were composed by university music students to highlight frequently found tonal patterns in music. Of course, the tonal pattern was extracted from the song below. Interestingly, the same treatment for rhythm patterns was not undertaken. That, I suppose, was in line with thought at the time that tonal elements were more important than rhythm elements. Now, as I understand it, research may have shifted such thought one-hundred eighty degrees.

Mason I hope not to such a drastic extent.

Kodály I developed a hierarchy of tonal patterns according to the frequency with which they are found in Hungarian folksongs. Therein is the basic difference between Professor Beattie's work and mine. And, while the American made no attempt to determine which, if any, rhythm patterns might be identified as extraordinary, I drafted simple rhythm patterns in duple meter that should become familiar to students. Research conducted over the past fifty years by a contemporary music psychologist, the same one who followed up on Carl Seashore's work in music aptitude, has discovered still a different approach. The implications for teaching to students' individual musical differences are enormous.

Orff Who is this person?

Kodály His name slips my mind, but Corybant mentioned his book.

To continue, three pattern difficulty levels were uncovered in his objective research: easy, moderately difficult, and difficult. To complete these studies, large groups of stratified, random samples of students of various ages across the United States were asked to listen to recorded tonal patterns and rhythm patterns and indicate whether two patterns in a series of pairs they heard sounded the same or different. If the two patterns in a pair were the same and if most students were aware they were, the pattern was considered easy. If patterns in a pair were the same, but approximately half the number of students were aware they were, the pattern was considered moderately difficult. If patterns in a pair were the same but only a few students were aware they were, the pattern was considered difficult. No analysis was undertaken for patterns in a pair that were different.

Because it was not possible for most teachers to find necessary research time or facilities to ask students to perform patterns, only difficulty levels of patterns in terms of audiation were studied. However, practice has found the majority of patterns easy for students to perform, read, and write are those they typically find easy to audiate, and the majority of patterns difficult for students to perform, read, and write are those they typically find difficult to audiate. It is hypothesized students cannot adequately learn to perform, read, and write patterns they cannot audiate.

However, if students can audiate a pattern, it does not necessarily mean they can automatically perform, read, or write it, because learning to perform, read, and write patterns involves learning skills they may not have acquired.

Jaques-Dalcroze Zoltán, how does this compare with your philosophy? The difficulty levels of tonal patterns you describe pertain to a diatonic, not an anhemitonic pentatonic, scale. If you embrace current findings, do you think your methodology will need to be attuned to it, no pun intended?

Kodály Êmile, my pedagogy was developed for Hungarian students, not for the world. I am pleased music educators in other countries have accepted it, but it might be good for some in their midst to conduct research on comparative difficulty levels of patterns indigenous to their culture, not excluding, of course, anhemitonic pentatonic patterns.

Mason What about a descending minor third being the universal interval of mankind? Do you believe that?

Kodály I did at one time. Maybe I still do, I'm not sure. I am in the throes of indecision because I cannot ignore what has been brought to my attention. Specifically, Donald Pond, after years of observational research in conjunction with the Pilsbury foundation, concluded a minor third is actually an integral part of speech chant. I cannot summarily dismiss that. If a falling minor third is in fact related to music, Mr. Pond suggests it would be indicative of Phrygian mode, or should I say, Phrygian tonality?

Orff What else?

Mason You made the statement half steps are the most difficult of intervals to sing. Did you imply half steps from "mi" to "fa" and "ti" to "do" are difficult to sing? Perhaps that is why you champion an anhemitonic pentatonic scale. And how does all that relate to audiating a resting tone?

Kodály The reference applies to chromatic alterations. More important, however, I find surprising the results of contemporary research that indicate difficulty levels of patterns have virtually no relation to the frequency with which the patterns are found in standard music literature.

Further, research undertaken more informally with small groups stipulate it is easier for students to audiate individual patterns than consecutive patterns, as in series, and it is easier for students to audiate tonal patterns incorporating large intervals than to perform those patterns. Stated in reverse, it is more difficult for students to audiate tonal patterns incorporating small intervals than to perform them. Even more worthy of note, and certainly more puzzling, is students find it easier to determine correctly two tonal patterns or two rhythm patterns sound the same than it is for them to determine patterns sound different.

Orff There is more to music than tonal patterns and rhythm patterns. When tonal and rhythm patterns are combined, music, as we know it, takes form. Zoltán, alluded to that before.

Kodály An important finding is worth repeating. Students are best taught to perform tonal patterns and rhythm patterns independently, so that every pitch in a tonal pattern is taught with the same duration, and every duration in a rhythm pattern is taught using the same pitch, but with inflection. Initial separation of tonal patterns and rhythm patterns is emphasized. Inchoate students struggle with understanding a tonal pattern combined with a rhythm pattern remains the same tonal pattern when combined with another rhythm pattern. Similarly, they find it thorny to understand a rhythm pattern combined with a tonal pattern remains the same rhythm pattern when combined with another tonal pattern.

Corybant That is in alignment with Piaget's theory of conservation, is it not?

Kodály I believe so. Moreover, it would be almost impossible to teach young children appropriately when tonal patterns and rhythm patterns are combined into melodic patterns. Only rarely can tonal and rhythm parts in a joint pattern share the same level of difficulty.

Jaques-Dalcroze If I may be a gadfly in the moment, I sense a glitch. In our discussion of the difficulty levels of tonal patterns and rhythm patterns, I have inferred all the while we are talking about degrees of ability to inner hear, retain, and understand them. Is that so?

Kodály Yes.

Jaques-Dalcroze Well, then let's talk about comparative difficulty levels of singing specific tonal patterns and chanting specific rhythm patterns. I am particularly interested in knowing the relationship of difficulty of inner hearing a pattern and performing that pattern. Is there a one-to-one relationship?

Seashore You have already explained that, Zoltán. He's talking about the correlation between listening and performing a given pattern.

Kodály Yes, thank you Carl, I am aware of that. As far as I know, such research has not been conducted, and if it has, I am oblivious of the results. As I have said, experimental research on difficulty levels of patterns was directed to audiation, not singing or moving, or, as a matter of fact, to instrumental performance.

Jaques-Dalcroze Zoltàn, I tip my cap to the researcher, but if I were you I would not alter my methodology until pertinent research is accomplished that offers more positive results.

Kodály What would you consider positive results? Do audiation and performance difficulty levels need to be exactly the same?

Jaques-Dalcroze I don't know. If they were found not complementary, how could that be balanced in an actual teaching situation?

XII: Patterns

Kodály That's not for me to presuppose.

Suzuki I remember there were music psychologists who engaged in research pertaining to tonal patterns, but they never became involved in developing academic curriculums. I forget names.

Kodály I call to mind one: Christian Paul Heinlein. I think he was associated with Johns-Hopkins University in Baltimore, Maryland. Carl Seashore, I'm sure you know of him. He was not flattering of your research in either music aptitude or overall music psychology.

Seashore True. He was an ardent critic, but some of his criticism was constructive. Or at least well taken. Another person, too, should be mentioned. His name is Otto Ortmann, but I don't know if he was associated with a university or not. Ortmann wrote an article, I believe in 1926, about the melodic relativity of tones.

Kodály Yes, I know. He, too, discovered it is easier for students to audiate individual patterns than consecutive than contiguous patterns. Although students find it easier to imitate an entire tonal pattern than to recall in audiation even the first pitch of a tonal pattern, they find the first pitch easier to recall than final or middle pitches. Middle pitches in a tonal pattern are most difficult for students to recall in audiation.

Albeit, there is an overall concept that has not been alluded to that I believe is important. Rhythm patterns are fundamental, and flexible enough, to be applied to all types of music. It is primarily rhythm patterns that establish and characterize style in music, be it early to post modern. When taught appropriately, rhythm patterns are not concretized in any one style.

Corybant What a session! I was thinking about the Peace of Augsburg, solidified in 1555, in which it was decreed religious toleration would be the code of behavior in all European geographical regions. Could we imagine a metaphor for ameliorating discordant opinions circling the earth about music pedagogy? How about calling it the Peace of Cybele? Just think, it could filter down to controversial zealots who entertain shimmering views. Now that would be something of which we all could be proud. Our friends in the earthly sphere would understand truth is not forever.

Go, dear friends. and engage yourselves in introspection.

XIII: Improvisation

Corybant We all agree that improvisation must be attended to next. I had intended to recommend that. So, let's begin.

I remember when we began our discussion of rhythm, we asked Zoltán, our resident linguist, to explain the etymology of the word "rhythm." Zoltán, will you now explain the source of the word "improvisation."

Kodály Of course. Improvisation is rooted in Latin *improvisus*, which translates to "not provided" or "not foreseen."

Suzuki That derivative meaning contrasts rather heavily with practices of imitation, memorization, and reading music notation, wouldn't you say?

Mason Yes, it does, but I think we should include the word "audiation" in that group. Remember, it has been said audiation is the basis of understanding intrinsic elements of music in comparison to extrinsic elements allied with simplistic emotional responses and programmatic associations. Now, I would like to take the concept of audiation further.

It seems dubious a student would be able to improvise without ability to audiate. True, persons can rely theoretically on scales and a mixture of practiced motifs and riffs, and thus claim they are improvising. In actuality, however, they are practicing in public, all the while quoting themselves over and over again. To accept that as musical improvisation is to say one who can repeat only memorized words is engaging in creative conversation. Persons who truly improvise spontaneously audiate what they are going to perform before they perform it.

Orff Do you mean if students cannot inner hear what is to be played on a music instrument before it is actually executed they are not improvising? What about vocal improvisation?

Jaques-Dalcroze I cannot imagine a singer improvising in a musical manner without knowing what is to be sung. And, yes, to your first question, Carl. Moreover, students should be capable of singing as well as inner hearing what they intend to improvise instrumentally. If not, they are simply exploring.

Kodály I agree with Émile. Carl, I admire the fact students following Orff pedagogy are not encumbered by studying music theory nor are forced to learn to read music notation before they are allowed to play an Orff mallet instrument. I know you refer to their performances as creativity, but in all due respect, in my opinion what they produce may be neither creativity nor improvisation. Lowell may be right when he suggests that specific activity may be exploration.

Suzuki May we discuss interrelationships of improvisation, imitation, memorization, and music reading?

Orff No, please, not yet. Émile's and Zoltàn have indirectly validated a salient point. I maintain what I proposed pedagogically is not a method. Methods destroy teachers' as well as children's creativity.

Now, to the main issue. It is true by removing bars for the fourth and seventh steps of a major scale from an xylophone, students' anhemitonic pentatonic creativity will not sound dissonant. Students develop confidence when they are continually reminded there are no mistakes. Whatever rhythms they invent in creative movement support borduns, that is, tonic and dominant roots, not a drone. Later, alternate intervals are introduced.

You know, using common Asian pentatonic tonality dissuades students from imitating familiar songs. But I still encourage imitation as a requisite for creativity. The sequence is from imitation to creativity within the realm of ostinati. Repetitive patterns provide students with a feeling of security, and those patterns encourage students to be creative, first rhythmically and then melodically. With regard to what supposedly is called exploration, Orff teachers are aware students need to acquire vocabularies of rhythm, melodic, and harmonic patterns to create and improvise with sophistication.

Mason An explanation of how Orff teachers guide students in acquiring those vocabularies would be helpful.

Kodály Yes, that would be instructive.

Orff You already know there is no standard method for these procedures. Each Orff teacher makes those decisions for herself or himself. For me, melodic patterns are derived from speech, and rhythm patterns from creative dance movement. In fact, both types of patterns influenced my composition, especially for musical theatre.

Suzuki Again, can we please return to a discussion of interrelationships of improvisation, imitation, memorization, and music reading?

Mason If we can agree audiation, or inner hearing, is fundamental, we can proceed with clarity. A student must engage in at least some imitation as readiness for audiation and improvisation and, of course, creativity. In that connection, I understand creativity is a readiness for improvisation. Whereas there are relatively few, if any, musical restrictions for creativity, improvisation is based on restrictions as in, for example, a harmonic progression or style. To some extent all creativity is a form of improvisation, and all improvisation is a form of creativity. The two exist on a continuum.

Suzuki What about memorization and music reading?

Mason Two straightforward answers. Research suggests one is either performing using memorization or audiation. Both cannot occur simultaneously. And for music reading, most music teachers are unaware when improvisation precedes reading in a student's education, reading may not even need to be taught. It will happen, be learned, naturally, because what is seen is audiated. Conversely, when students are taught to read music notation by decoding symbols without learning to notationally audiate, it takes an abundance of time to force them through the reading process. If truth be known, they never actually learn to read, but only to follow directions. They are bereft of audiation. Anyone who might not be shocked by what I have said actually does not understand what I have said.

Suzuki Lowell, do you truly believe music reading need not be taught if one can improvise?

Mason Perhaps a hyperbole, but what I said is more fact than fiction.

Jaques-Dalcroze Improvisation is not limited to performance. No two persons listen to or read the same piece of music the same way. Consider how many conductors interpret a score differently. That becomes joyfully obvious upon comparative listening to ensembles they direct. Also, think of performers who, with acquired maturity, change their interpretation of a piece of music over time. I'm thinking specifically of Glenn Gould's various performances of the *Goldberg Variations*.

Furthermore, as all professional musicians know, many crucially sensitive parts of music cannot be notated. Thus, we all are improvising no matter how we are relating to music, sometimes through necessity and other times not. Unfortunately, importance of improvisation has been grossly misunderstood, if not ignored.

Suzuki What do you mean?

Jaques-Dalcroze If you ask why so many musicians do not or cannot improvise, the answer is, if I may jest, they took lessons. When persons ask me how I might recommend they learn to improvise, I tell them to gain practical experience, make brave fools of themselves until they become somewhat accomplished, and above all, avoid academic classes and theoretical explanations. Most, if not all, great composers first improvised what they wrote, and instrumentalists were expected

XIII: Improvisation

to improvise cadenzas. Certainly none took instruction in the art. Ironically, most contemporary musicians are oblivious to the detail first endings historically were not always intended as instructions to repeat a section. It was expected, after being familiar with a section of a composition, orchestral players would improvise solo and in ensemble a contrasting but related section of the same length and conclude with an appropriate second ending.

Suzuki But Émile, you gave lessons, did you not?

Corybant I must interrupt. Please tell me if what I have learned is or is not flawed. As I understand it, there are various ways to improvise in singing and instrumental performance. The four most popular approaches are first, performing variations of a melody in the same or different styles; second, performing scale patterns associated with chord symbols; third, performing original melodies superimposed on a progression of harmonic patterns; and fourth, performing a progression of original harmonic patterns that support a melody.

In the first approach, a musician stylistically performs variations of a melody without necessarily being conscious of the progression of harmonic patterns that forms the foundation of the melody. In the second approach, a musician performs melodic fragments based on scales associated with chords. In the third approach, a melody is improvised over a progression of harmonic patterns in much the same way it was done using figured bass during the Baroque era, so the progression of harmonic patterns directs the performer in improvising a melody. In the fourth approach, a melody directs a performer in improvising a progression of harmonic patterns.

Jaques-Dalcroze I don't think any of us would disagree with that.

Corybant Thank you.

Jaques-Dalcroze Carl has explained how Orff teachers engage in improvisation. I agree wholeheartedly with him. Direct experience is the crucible. I taught dance improvisation, and I want to explain a few ideas associated with my overall method, yes method. It comprises three independent elements: movement, ear training, and improvisation. With regard to the latter, my students respond to the slightest gradations in time, intensity, duration, and phrasing as they improvise using their bodies while standing and moving around the room. To stimulate students, I stood at the piano while improvising.

By the way, my style of teaching is now popular in other arts, not only music—dance, ballet, and theatre. Everyone knew I hated the ascetic Reformation that took place in the 16th century. My pedagogy reflected freedom and zest for life, and that made it attractive. Eurhythmics gained cosmic acceptance as a type of therapy, and it also proved suitable for teaching blind persons. Thanks to Wolff Dohrn, a German industrialist, who helped me found Hellerau, I was given precious time to develop and transmit my thoughts to teachers and students.

von Laban I empathize with your appreciation for assistance from persons who understood the value of your work. I, too, had a similar experience. Soon after I immigrated to England, an estate in Addlestone was to donated to my group for the express purpose of studying behavioral needs of industrial workers and psychiatric patients.

Orff Rudolf, did you know Orff teaching in the United States of America is also available to those in need of therapy?

von Laban Yes, and that pleases me.

Kodály Some Kodály teachers guide their students in melodic improvisation, as in the second type of improvisation Corybant described. Initially students use pitches. First, only "so" and "mi" are performed. "La" is added after students have had ample opportunity to contrast functions of "do" and "la."

Suzuki I am particularly interested in the third type of improvisation Corybant mentioned.

XIII: Improvisation

Corybant A harmonic pattern is much like a tonal pattern, except a tonal pattern includes only one part and a harmonic pattern includes two or more simultaneously sounding parts. Just as individual pitches in tonal patterns progress from one to the next, a harmonic pattern includes triads or chords progressing from one to the next. The overall sound—sonance—of a progression of harmonic patterns in relation to a tonality and keyality gives overall contextual meaning to harmonic patterns.

Suzuki Is that all?

Corybant There is more, but I wasn't sure anyone was interested.

Kodály Speaking for all of us, we would appreciate your continuing.

Corybant Actually, there is research which supports the views I will be conveying. Perhaps most compelling to me, and I suspect particularly to anyone who has not thought much about improvisation or has been steeped in music theory, is the following. The vertical structure of chords, positions of individual pitches making up chords, is extraneous to sonance of a harmonic pattern. When chords are taught that way, the emphasis is on music theory and rules of part writing. However, when chords are taught in linear fashion, as collectively constituting a harmonic pattern and ultimately harmonic progressions, all relating to a tonality and keyality, emphasis is on musical context. Whether chords are in root position or in inversion is irrelevant to the context of the harmonic pattern to which the chords belong.

Suzuki Anything else?

Corybant Yes. There are four levels of ability in audiating—using the word "audiation" loosely—chord progressions. First, some persons are unaware chord changes are taking place as they listen to a melody. Others are aware chord changes are taking place as they listen to a melody, but they cannot identify the actual changes, that is, the chord letter names or symbols representing the chords, even after they have heard the chords performed. Third, some persons are aware chord changes are taking place as they listen to a melody and they can identify the actual changes only after they have heard the chords performed. Fourth, the most advanced level, includes persons who can anticipate chords that will be performed before they actually hear them. Sometimes chords performed are splendid substitutes for the original harmony.

Jaques-Dalcroze I suspect professional improvisers achieve the highest level. What about students whose achievement is commensurate with the first three levels?

Corybant Interesting! Now we are circling back to students' individual musical differences and needs. So many music educators let that pass without a whimper.

Before I attend to that, I must tell you what prevents so many students from participating in harmonic improvisation. It is not only their inability to respond to chord progressions. It is also their lack of rhythm achievement. The second and third types of aspiring improvisers fall into this group. Although those students are convinced chord changes will occur, they cannot predict when a chord change will actually take place in an ongoing melody. In fact, often they cannot even hear changes in a chord progression. Oddly, these students have not learned to coordinate their breathing and movement with their audiation of chord changes. Fundamentals of ongoing rhythm elude them.

Jaques-Dalcroze If your speaking about harmonic rhythm, that doesn't surprise me.

Corybant Now, in teaching to students' individual musical differences in terms of improvisational skill, attentive teachers are knowledgeable about the comparative difficulty levels of chord patterns and sequence them in instruction like they sequence difficulty levels of tonal patterns and rhythm patterns. There are two tests that you should know about, the Harmonic Improvisation Readiness Record and

Rhythm Improvisation Readiness Record. When used with a valid music aptitude test, students' results can be of enormous value to their teachers in improvisation instruction. Whether or not you are comfortable with testing, even a cursory examination of the corresponding test manuals will kindle both your synchronic and diachronic speculation.

Suzuki Thank you, Corybant.

Corybant We all have had a cognitive workout.

XIV: Teaching, Learning, and Curriculum

Corybant I am concerned I might not have been accurate in reporting what I have read about improvisation, so I suggest you examine the original research reports yourselves. There is much I either did not understand or have forgotten. I would be delighted to offer titles of some books. All are in contemporary bibliographies.

Mason Corybant, I did take time to search out some manuscripts you recommended. Thank you for suggesting we do so.
    You used the words "synchronic" and "diachronic" toward the end of our previous meeting. Is it possible two other words were looming in your mind at the time because of their interrelationships?

Corybant Which two words?

Mason "Phylogenetic" and "ontogenetic."

Corybant A bit of a leap. If you remember, Carl Orff sides with the latter. Carl, am I correct in saying, in terms of education, you are more interested in concentrating on a person's individual musical development from birth through adulthood rather than acquainting a person with the development of music historically?

Orff That sums up a portion of my philosophy.

Mason I came across a sentence in my reading that, at least to me, is a conundrum.

Orff What is it?

Mason "Music is audiated as hinged mosaic relationships linked to networks of comparative pattern structures." Who can translate that?

Corybant I will try by examining the three parts separately.

Hinged mosaic relationships refer to tonality, keyality, meter, and tempo, among other elements, such as interpretation and phrasing, interrelated in a melody. They are inseparable, not always distinguishable from one another, as in a montage, when one is audiating an artistic piece of music.

Networks are links connecting elements, much like the way synapses connect brain cells. Connections are like spider webs, each chamber having a multitude of conjunctions traveling in every which way.

Comparative pattern structures constitute the same and different tonal, rhythm, and harmonic patterns comprising a piece of music. When patterns are audiated as being different, but related to one another as well as to the Gestalt of a composition, incomparable understanding and enjoyment are patently gifted to performers as well as to listeners. Identification of difference always trumps recognition of sameness.

Mason What you explained, I presume, is an explanation of audiation.

Corybant In a way. However, I suggest you all read my explanation several times in the transcript of our symposium. Or, better yet, go to the original source. If you do either, I believe once you are comfortable with the thoughts, they will contribute to a thorough understanding of audiation.

Is there a theme for this session?

Seashore I think it would now be good to hear more about audiation.

XIV: Teaching, Learning, and Curriculum

Kodály Carl, can you read about it instead? I would rather we entertain a new topic. I wonder how the group feels about that?

Jaques-Dalcroze What would you suggest?

Kodály I think it would be beneficial to give more attention to teaching and learning. The difference between the two is something to which I should have given much more thought. I am fascinated with the subject

Seashore I've been doing a great deal of thinking about teaching and learning. Though I am probably not the most qualified as an educator, I will begin anyway. I did experimental research on education, and am obliquely in touch with current practices.

    We have been told teachers teach and students learn. Quality of students' learning is directly related to quality of teaching they receive. Extraordinary education is a result of teachers understanding how students learn. To teach without understanding or concern about how students learn results in less than acceptable teaching. Regardless, many teachers teach lacking that knowledge. Teacher education programs, not so much music teachers themselves, are to blame. Methods and teaching techniques courses in colleges and universities are legion, but learning courses are a rare event, uncommon as a rooster's egg.

Mason Carl, students' ability to generalize should be the embodiment of education. Students must generalize in order to learn. The ability to teach oneself, once achieved, carries on throughout adulthood. It is a mark of an educated person. Teaching students solely to imitate and memorize falls far short of the mark. Students who can generalize are also able to make inferences.

Seashore And students who make inferences are the most creative in society, overall. They have been educated, not trained.

Mason Further, musical creativity points the way to facility in improvisation.

Suzuki All of this sounds good. But is this simply idealism, or can it become reality? And, if it can become reality, how is it accomplished?

Orff Despite my reputation of promoting laissez-faire pedagogy, I want to attempt to answer Shinicki with something new.

Corybant Are some of us beginning to think about change?

Kodály Let's not say "change." Imposing change can restrict freedom of thought.

Seashore Zoltán reminds me of a statement by George Bernard Shaw: "It is easier to move a cemetery than to change the mind of a teacher."

Corybant Enough. Carl, let's talk about teaching and learning.

Orff I have not changed my mind about my pedagogical philosophy. What I am saying is our discussions have caused me to think about new ideas. Where I will go with them is uncertain.

Kodály Go on, Carl, go on.

Orff As you remember from when we talked about preparatory audiation and audiation, we have five music vocabularies. In sequential order of their ideal development, they are listening, performing, audiation and improvisation, reading, and writing. Their sequence and order outlines how music is learned. When teachers ignore this, learning, in most cases, comes to a virtual standstill. Unfortunately, teaching supercedes learning. A plethora of imitation, memorization, and explanations of music theory replaces the ideal sequence of learning music. Unfortunately, many teachers assume they are left with no choice in the matter.

Mason Why?

Seashore Because so many children attend school with impoverished musical backgrounds. There is not sufficient curricular time to teach students as obvious common sense and research direct. Music educators do the best they can by taking shortcuts.

Kodály What about improvisation?

Orff That question is easily answered by asking oneself why so few musicians, professional and otherwise, improvise.

Suzuki But Zoltán and I see imitation and memorization inherent to our teaching.

Mason Shinicki, I have profound respect for both you and Zoltán. True, you generally begin with listening and then move on to performance, but the remaining three vocabularies appear to be circumvented. Imitation and memorization preempt audiation and improvisation, and thus, students don't learn notational audiation. Reading is taught in terms of deciphering. I'm not sure about writing. In a word, students rarely cross the bridge from imitation to audiation. A simple and obvious solution for most teachers would be to reevaluate their belief in the beneficial effects of memorization and note reading.

Orff Perhaps your being a little harsh, Lowell.

Mason Perhaps so.

Seashore Let's try another tack. Think of four words: "what," "why," "when," and "how." First we ask, what should students be taught? Naturally, various answers should be expected from a variety of teachers. Nonetheless, once the question is answered, the next question is, why are we teaching what we are teaching? Unless the second question can be answered intelligently and with confidence, the answer to the first question is inappropriate and a new answer to the first question is needed.

The third question gets to the heart of learning. When should students be exposed to individual parts of an established curriculum? In other words, what is the sequence and order of presentation of learning components in terms of the five vocabularies? The fourth question of how bears on methods and techniques. Both constitute teaching. The third question is most important and the fourth, in my opinion, is least important. If comprehensive sequential learning formed the foundation of curriculums using the many superlative ideas embedded in Orff and Kodály classroom music methodologies, music education could rise to new heights.

Kodály I am so pleased, Carl, you used the word "curriculum." A sequential curriculum is bedrock in pursuit of excellence in education and yet, many music educators avoid it.

Orff Yes, I've heard music teachers say if they were bound by a curriculum, their artistic freedom would be jeopardized.

Kodály Nonsense. They masquerade unpreparedness as creativity.

Suzuki I've seen music curriculums in many schools I visited.

Kodály Shinicki, a curriculum is not an anthologies of songs accompanied by teaching suggestions. Did you observe any sequence and order in the documents, or were they plans outlining specific songs to be taught for holidays? Perhaps songs and recordings were selected to coincide with historical and patriotic material being taught in other subjects.

Mason And what about methods books for instrumental music instruction? I'm not objecting to what they are called, but I am saying their function can be reduced to merely practices for developing instrumental technique.

Is there sequence and order in developing instrumental technique?

XIV: Teaching, Learning, and Curriculum

Suzuki Yes, yes, yes. I devoted my professional life to that end.

Mason But, Shinicki, my crucial question is, how do you unite audiation to developing instrumental technique?

Suzuki That occurs naturally, by divine intervention.

Corybant Funny, yes, but let's back off a minute. Shinicki, tell us about your friendship with Albert Einstein?

Suzuki We often played chamber music at home. Albert, though not a great musician, enjoyed playing violin. He would interject pithy remarks when they were least expected. For example, possibly to assuage his musical boundaries, he once commented teachers for whom English was a second language taught English better than native speakers. He then went on to say that might not be the case with musicians. Whereas foreign teachers usually know English grammar better than native speakers, and that probably works to their advantage, the contrary seems to be the case with music teachers. They are incapacitated by too much music theory. My favorite of Einstein's maxims is, "Great spirits always encounter violent opposition from mediocre minds."

Kodály We are missing a decisive component of learning: early childhood music.

Orff I agree, completely.

Seashore We cannot afford to discuss music curriculum and exclude the vital role of music education in early childhood. I helped found the child welfare research station at the University of Iowa which was designed to cater to preschool children. Although music teachers were among the faculty, music was not of central concern. I've since thought a lot about that endeavor.

   Imagine, for a moment, you did not hear or speak your native language until you entered school at five or six years old. Your teachers, nevertheless, expected you to ask and answer questions and to learn to read and write along with your classmates who had been exposed to language from the moment they were born, prenatally notwithstanding.

Now, think about learning music in school. For many children, a similar situation is real. They never learned to develop a music listening vocabulary, which is necessary for pragmatic and rational future learning about music. Children are asked to sing without having experienced the difference between their speaking and singing voices. More absurdly, they are expected to learn to read what they cannot audiate or, if you prefer, inner hear. Their limitations are exacerbated by formal instruction, primarily because they are not ready to learn what the music teacher is attempting to teach.

Jaques-Dalcroze Carl, how would you respond to a parent who says contemporary children constantly hear music through media? That should automatically develop their listening vocabulary, so they don't need special informal music guidance in preschool?

Seashore I would ask it is acceptable to them to have their child learn his or her native language by listening to recordings? I think not. Without one-to-one personal relationship and eye contact, the child would never develop sufficient language skill to achieve in school.

Kodály Carl, tell us, how might such a situation be remedied when a child enters school?

Seashore I must say it cannot. Remedial instruction is not possible. The option is compensatory instruction, and it should be understood children who require compensatory instruction will never achieve at a level they could have if they enjoyed informal guidance in music at an early age. Informal guidance received at home is requisite for advantageously responding to formal instruction in school. Notice the difference between the terms "informal guidance" and "formal instruction."

XIV: *Teaching, Learning, and Curriculum*

Orff I am aware there are band, orchestra, and choir teachers who also teach early childhood music.

Seashore That is admirable, providing they are not teaching toddlers as if they were little kindergartners. I am not casting aspersions, but many music teachers are not knowledgeable about the needs of children younger than eighteen months. You know, the amount and extent of what children learn naturally from birth to three years will never again be possible. Musically speaking, for most children, that opportunity is unconsciously forsaken.

Callous as it may sound, it is my conviction the most opportune time to learn to respond honestly to music beyond simplistic emotional reactions vanishes after three years of age. Children who have not engaged in preparatory audiation before they enter school at age five are effectively "over the hill."

Mason Qualified early childhood teachers should be given more respect and paid more highly than teachers in secondary schools and professors. Rewards in educational institutions resemble an inverted pyramid. Teachers in higher education and professors receive preferential treatment over elementary school and preschool teachers who garner little attention, consideration, and esteem.

Kodály I often thought a more proper title for professors might be "confessors." You know, if all children were given an appropriate early childhood music education, higher music education may be gratuitous? Parents, the most natural and capable teachers, might become all that is necessary.

Corybant Have we completed our dialogue about teaching, learning, and music curriculums? We certainly have strayed a bit.

Kodály Corybant, I need a little more time.

Corybant Please take whatever time you need, Zoltán.

Kodály The enormous value of students learning individual patterns is not to be denied. Patterns are fundamental to music. But think of language. Children learn to use individual words at about one year old. Soon after, they begin to listen to and speak more than one word at a time. They move from content—single words—to context—phrases and sentences. The same path must be followed in music guidance and instruction. Of course, in the beginning there are individual patterns, but it is critical children be guided informally and late-comers instructed formally in chaining patterns. In that manner, they will become conscious of the contextual centrality of a resting one, that is, a tonal center.

Turning phrases not to be disregarded, series of multiple patterns are the essence of music, and they can be taught none too soon. And, what I have said supports the initial need to teach tonal patterns and rhythm patterns separately. They become too complex for new learners when combined into melodic patterns prematurely. I must emphasize, it seems feasible students should learn tonal patterns and rhythm patterns apart from one another as readiness for singing melodic patterns. Be clear: songs comprise melodic patterns. At the very least, multiple patterns might be taught concurrently with songs.

von Laban Thanks, Zoltán. Time permitting, I would not object to devoting an entire session to the importance of acquiring multiple—series of—patterns in all five music vocabularies. I'm convinced the reason so many musicians cannot improvise is because they focus on individual notes, if not individual patterns, and have not come to grips with audiating pattern continuity. Context escapes them, and that loss is debilitating for developing the third music vocabulary.

Orff Interesting thoughts.

von Laban What stands out in my mind is that not being able to inner hear series and layers of rhythm patterns may be the major contributor to arrhythmia. So many of my students had this malady. They needed to be re-membered. I insert a hyphen because I refer to their body parts. As young babies, body parts move naturally in smooth combination with one another. Societal manifestations steal that capability, and it is now a chore for teachers to assist them in "membering" them so that they combine their body parts again in the way nature originally intended.

Corybant Are there more comments before we adjourn?

Please bring whatever thoughts you might put together to our next meeting.

XV: Timbre/Range Preference

Corybant Amazing! We did not arrange a time to reassemble, but we are all here.

Mason Corybant, I think I may speak for all of us. There is so much benefit in honest and sincere interactions of philosophies and opinions. Egos seem to be less troublesome, perhaps even not apparent at all, in our present existence.

Corybant Knowing what I do about you all, I would have expected nothing less than mutual respect. Gentlemen, one and all.

Now, turning to matters at hand, I must tell you about an interesting experience I had a celestial moon cycle ago. Cybele did not summon me, and I was curious as to why she had not called me. I found her resting. She inquired about the progress of our convention, as she called it. In the middle of my report she interrupted me and related a charming story she had recently heard.

As an incredibly young girl, Jacqueline du Pré, the English cellist who established the legendary and definitive interpretation of Edward Elgar's cello concerto in E minor, attended a concert with her parents. Immediately upon hearing the cello being played, she stated emphatically that was the instrument she must learn to play. She would not hear of any other instrument recommended by local teachers. They believed her physical structure would limit her achievement. Finally she was given a small cello. Lessons began, and thank goodness for that. The point Cybele made was most persons, especially musicians, have a preference for a specific tone quality, possibly even more than one. She asked if I agreed. Before I could answer, she requested I put the question to the group. In the meantime, I scouted out existing research. Of course, if you do not believe the topic is worth your time and speculation, we can choose another. That being the case, I will pass on my personal thoughts to Cybele.

Jaques-Dalcroze I think it is a splendid topic. In that connection, I taught composition to Ernest Bloch, a Swiss American who wrote a cello concerto titled *Schelmo*, the Hebrew name for Solomon. As he was conceiving that rhapsodic work, he silently heard the cello. He never questioned that it might be written for another instrument. No other would do. Preference for tone quality and range of the cello for him was not a determining contumely.

Suzuki Aren't most composers more eclectic than that?

Kodály I suspect so, but I think they prefer certain instrumental sounds. Obversely, I seem to remember Mozart disdained the flute.
   Corybant, we all undoubtedly have personal, that is, subjective, preferences and anecdotes to relate, but I think it would be most productive if you begin by telling us about objective research you encountered concerning timbre.

Corybant Zoltán, is there a difference between them? Timbre and tone quality?

Kodály In popular parlance, no, but theoretically yes. The word "timbre" came into use in the late 18ᵗʰ century. It meant an anonymous melody used with different texts, earlier in connection with liturgical chants. In the middle ages it signified a small drum or tambourine. Currently, timbre is used by some psycho-acousticians to describe the relative strengths of harmonic, and occasionally non-harmonic, frequencies present in a sound wave.

Corybant How does timbre compare to the term "tone quality."

Kodály Theoretically, tone quality refers to temperament of a sound as distinct from its pitch. It distinguishes resonance of one music instrument or voice from another. Despite that, timbre and tone quality currently are typically used interchangeably.

Corybant Thank you, Zoltán. So many terms used in music are willy-nilly borrowed from other disciplines, and so few musicians understand their original and manifold meanings.

Cybele's question inspired me. After consulting several sources, I consider the manual for the Instrument Timbre/Range Preference Test to offer the most current information in a concise manner. Objective research in the United States reveals importance of timbre and range of a music instrument are second only to music aptitude as significant factors in students' success in instrumental music. Students become motivated and successful when they learn to play with good tone quality on a music instrument that has a timbre and range they like. When students' Instrument Timbre/Range Preference Test scores are combined with their scores on a valid music aptitude test, as much as 65% of the reason or reasons for their success in school instrumental music can be predicted after only one year of instruction. When scores on a valid music aptitude test are used alone, however, predictive validity decreases by about 10%.

Jaques-Dalcroze Do all students have timbre and range preference?

Corybant No. About 20% do not. About the same percentage have multiple preferences.

What I find most disturbing, however, is regardless of whether they do or do not indicate a timbre/range preference, almost 50% of students in fourth and fifth grades who score above the 80th percentile on a valid music aptitude test do not volunteer to study a music instrument. Thus, along with the Instrument Timbre/Range Preference Test, a valid music aptitude test might be given to all students in every classroom to identify those musically gifted students who should be encouraged to participate in instrumental music instruction. Timbre and range preferences, however, will not compensate for modest music aptitude.

Suzuki I recall we talked about physical characteristics and success in learning to play a music instrument.

Jaques-Dalcroze We did. I don't think a person's size and shape should be ignored when choosing a music instrument. However, a more persuasive consideration might be a student's preference for timbre and range of a music instrument.

Aside from the point, I would like to know what the content is of the timbre and range preference test Corybant has made reference to. How can such a test reveal a student's preference? It would seem to me if a student is given an opportunity to hear a variety of music instruments played by accomplished performers, certainly a reasoned choice can be made. In that case, a test should prove unessential.

Corybant What you say, Émile, is logical, but from what I have learned, it is unreasonable. Think of it this way.

Synthesized sounds are used in the test rather than actual sounds of music instruments for one essential reason. The same melody is repeated in paired timbres and ranges in a series of questions, and students indicate whether they prefer the first or second rendition in each pair. If consistency of choice is evident, that specifies a preferred timbre and range.

Jaques-Dalcroze So?

Corybant It was uncovered in prepublication developmental research studies of the Instrument Timbre/Range Preference Test that when actual sounds of music instruments are used, validity of the test is sacrificed. Why? Because many students indicate a preference for sound of an actual music instrument simply because it is familiar and therefore it can be associated with friends who play or will be learning to play that instrument. Further, they chose to identify with popular musicians who play the instrument, or they are attracted to the size and appearance of the instrument. Also, wearing a uniform, attending sports events, and possibility of being a participant in band and orchestra trips is a persuasive factor. Finally, whether the instrument is owned by the school or its rental or purchase is a necessity is highly influential in making a choice. Unfortunately, timbre and range is of little conscious concern to them. Thus, to assure the validity of preference, there seems to be no alternative to using synthesized sounds.

Seashore Are there limitations to such a test?

Corybant It is not possible to achieve a full spectrum for timbre and range using a synthesizer.

Mason Please, would someone be kind enough to explain a synthesizer?

Corybant It is an electronic instrument, usually played with a keyboard, that combines simple waveforms to produce complex synthetic sounds unlike those produced by an actual music instrument.

Kodály Practical reasons have been explained for using synthesized sounds. Are there technical and pedagogical reasons as well?

Seashore Let me guess. It is not possible for different, or even the same, musicians to perform the same short melody on different music instruments with the same musical expression. Also, from a standpoint of test reliability and validity, it would not have been prudent, if feasible, to increase the length of the test so as to include all different stylistic tone qualities—such as commercial, studio, symphonic, and jazz—for each music instrument on the recording. If only one actual sound were presented, it might be one some students would not like, even though they prefer another actual sound associated with a given instrument. In that regard, use of vibrato would further complicate the problem.

Corybant You're on target, Carl. That's what I remember reading.

Mason It occurs to me most of us in the group perform on a keyboard instrument, piano or organ. Is there any implication in that observation?

Suzuki I play piano, but only as an amateur. Nevertheless, I prefer the sound of strings, preferably violin.

Kodály I think you are fortunate. There have been times I wished I played an additional instrument, one with tone quality and range that also has appeal to me.

Corybant It is reported that a sizeable number of professional musicians wish they played an alternate instrument, not because it might have been easier to learn but because they liked its engaging tone quality and range characteristics.

I think I neglected to tell you something else. I can't wait to tell Cybele. She will be amused. Research indicates why most young school students choose a specific music instrument to study. You might think the reason is because of parental wishes, the family owns the music instrument, the school provides the music instrument and therefore it need not be bought or rented, the band or orchestra director suggested it, or a friend or famous person plays it. None of those. In the majority of cases, the school bus driver makes the decision, depending upon whether he or she will it allow it on the school bus for the trip to and from school.

Mason That doesn't show much respect for the music faculty.

Suzuki When asked to give a definition of a string quartet, the responder said, "Someone who can play the violin, someone who cannot play the violin, someone who used to play the violin, and someone who detests the violin."

Corybant Delightful!
Carl Seashore, what do you think?

Seashore I am grateful importance of timbre and range preference finally has been uncovered objectively. How times have changed! I find it difficult, however, to imagine how I would fare as a teacher under present-day circumstances.

Mason Interesting. You say, Corybant, only few students choose to learn a music instrument because they like the sound of its timbre and range.

Corybant As a matter of fact, most students never have heard a variety of music instruments played by professionals except, perhaps, the one their music teacher plays. It is said most music majors do not hear what individual music instruments sound like when played by a professional until they enter college or conservatory.

Seashore I believe that has always been the case in the United States of America, but I'm not sure about other countries. You know, it's a shame so many students do not continue to study a music instrument. The dropout rate is enormous. Recent figures indicate by the end of the second year of beginning instrumental music instruction, less than 10% of students remain in the school program.

Kodály The primary reason for that dismal finding may be because students do not audiate an appropriate tone quality to produce on their music instrument. Also, although they may be able to audiate an attractive tone quality, they may not have learned technically how to produce it on a music instrument. Professional musicians, exceptional soloists in particular, inevitably audiate the tone quality they actually wish to hear before beginning to perform.

Suzuki Yes, that dropout rate is not totally because so many students learn to play a music instrument for which they lack a timbre and range preference. I maintain it is poor teaching. Also, many students lack inner hearing or audiation readiness to be successful in playing a music instrument. For example, they cannot sing what they intend to play.

Jaques-Dalcroze Who's fault is that?

Suzuki Classroom music teachers' as well as instrumental directors'. And, don't forget, many parents don't take responsibility for encouraging children to sing and practice, and indeed, for overseeing practice sessions. That, however, is not the case in Suzuki instruction. Parents know from the beginning they are to play a vital part in the child's learning. That is why the program is so successful.

Seashore If students achieve at a higher level when they are learning to play a music instrument for which they have timbre and range preferences, obviously they maintain an interest in instrumental music study.

Corybant Yes, of course, the dropout rate for those students is less than for students who select a music instrument fancifully or arbitrarily. There is a statistically significant difference in dropout rate between the two groups. Less than the 20% who make a wise choice based on timbre and range preference discontinue instrumental instruction after two years.

Jaques-Dalcroze What is a statistically significant difference?

Seashore A difference is statistically significant when the superiority in achievement of one group or the benefit of a medication, for example, is supported objectively when compared to another. Different levels of assurance may be used. For example, if you want to be almost incontrovertibly sure, the one-percent level of confidence is used. When a statistically significant difference is established at that level, it means if the experiment were repeated one hundred times under the same conditions and with similar students, the difference found would occur by chance only one time in a hundred. On the other hand, the level of confidence need not to be so stringent. Thus, the five-percent level of confidence might be employed. Given a statistically significant result, chance occurrences would arise in five of one hundred repetitions.

By the way, no significant difference does not indicate there is no real difference. The null hypothesis can only be rejected or retained, never accepted. That is, it cannot be proved.

Orff What is the null hypothesis?

Seashore It is a mathematical test of whether the difference between two means is of any consequence. When the null hypothesis is rejected, the resultant mean difference is significant. When the mean difference is not significant, the null hypothesis is not accepted. It is retained until further research is undertaken which may reveal the previous conclusion invalid. Logistically, there can never be no real difference.

Corybant Thank you Carl. That style of research seems to have advantages, but I am sure it courts limitations as well.

Seashore Undeniably.

Corybant Will a discussion of research be our next topic?

XVI: Research

Corybant I peeked in on some revelry at Cybele's court a few minutes ago. I saw one of her sycophants in the entourage sitting alone. In the course of our conversation, I was reminded not much time remains for our group to stay intact. Soon each of you will journey in a new sphere. But let's not allow that to hinder our attitudes. What I'm saying is, I think this will need to be our penultimate session. The next, our final one, will be directed to sharing our goodwill and good-byes.

Mason Will we have an opportunity to gather again?

Corybant I'm not sure. It requires more complex calculations than I can do.

Jaques-Dalcroze Can someone else do them? What about Einstein?

Corybant No, unfortunately he's on another mission. Something to do with global warming, I think.

Orff Corybant, if you fortuitously happen to discover us all in the same sphere some time in the future, will you chance a way for us to meet again?

Corybant That is a certainty, and I shall attempt to gather others to join our group.

Kodály Not to question your judgment, Corybant, but I would like to suggest you not make the group too large. A seminar is one thing; a convention, something else entirely,

von Laban Corybant, I want to tell you how much I appreciate your organizing and assembling the group.

Suzuki Yes, Rudolf speaks for all of us.

Mason May we dedicate this current conversation to a discussion of research? I am not interested at the moment in research results, but I want to know more about research techniques and related philosophical issues that have evolved over time. I am not sure of all that has taken place and what changes have occurred since my taking leave of earth.

Corybant Lowell, these are topics of vital interest to us all. Are there any objections?

Jaques-Dalcroze I, for one, have none, except the proviso that we mix compelling professional interests with personal themes if we wish. We have a little time.

Corybant We must keep this discussion brief. Where and with whom do we begin? I plead uncertainty.

Seashore Because my experience seems to be unique, I think it best to begin with what I know, or rather, what I knew on earth.

Corybant Please go on. I presume you'll discuss research that has taken place after Lowell's death?

Seashore More than two millennia ago, Aristotle maintained the best path to knowledge was through deductive thought. It began with a general premise, moved to a minor premise, and ended with a specific conclusion.

Mason I knew that already.

XVI: Research

Seashore But all may not.

For example, all professors are intelligent. Samuel is a professor. Therefore, Samuel is intelligent. During the 17th and 18th centuries, the Enlightenment, natural philosophical research separated itself from philosophical research, thereby challenging deductive reasoning and replacing it with a new type of scientific inquiry, inductive reasoning. The latter, with murmurs of protest, has prevailed to the present time. Research replaced re-search, that is, bibliographically studying yesteryear practices and events time and time again. Please note, I emphasized a separation in the word "research," inserting a hyphen between "re" and "search." There is a difference, you know, between history and historiography.

Jaques-Dalcroze I detect a bit of derision.

Seashore Inductive reasoning begins with specifics and moves to the general, in contrast to deductive reasoning which begins with the general and moves to the specific. For example, when comparing language acquisition of two intact groups of children taught with different methodologies it is discovered one group learned more than the other, the inductive generalization made is all children resembling the providential group who participated in the research might best be taught using the superior method. For a variety of reasons, however, it is implicitly clear neither doctrinal deductive nor inductive reasoning is efficacious for engaging in music education research, although inductive approaches often serve useful purposes in medical, agricultural, therapeutic, and scientific laboratory research.

Mason Carl, please be specific. What reasons?

Seashore Inductive reasoning has spawned convoluted and intricate research designs in the social sciences. They are heavily saturated with elaborate statistical analyses and tests of probability touted as ideal for comparing, for example, resultant differences among students who are exposed to different methodologies. Although the procedures look good and appealing on paper, it was my experience that without large numbers of students and willing capable teachers, actual use of recommended statistical designs and methods would be hasty and rash.

One reason is without large numbers of students to assure randomness, or without stratified random samples of smaller numbers of students from whom results are to be generalized, it becomes pointless to pursue such research. Results will indubitably be inconclusive.

Another reason is, when comparing various methods, all teachers must be equally competent and well versed in the one or more methods they are teaching. That condition can only rarely, if ever, be met. Because that requirement is more ideal than real, and thus, impractical and hardly ever satisfied, the need to disregard protocol and engage teachers who do not share comparable expertise to instruct students using specific methods is inevitable. Because of these limitations I necessarily accomplished most of my analyses using correlation techniques.

Corybant Is that it?

Seashore I have a bit more. To further aggravate the situation, statistical analyses, such as t-tests, F-tests, and Chi-square tests, analysis of variance, multivariate analysis, and factor analysis are used to examine data to determine if derived differences or relationships are statistically significant or attributable to chance. Textbook technicians forewarn these tests have at least three preliminary assumptions that must be affirmed. For example, individual students, not classrooms of students, must be randomly selected and assigned to a specific method. All groups should begin at the same average level of academic accomplishment related to what is being studied and to criteria used to determine if differences do in fact exist after instruction. Each group should have a normal distribution of students in terms of high, average, and low achievers in the subject and methods being examined.

Mason Is such preliminary protocol really necessary?

XVI: Research

Seashore So it is said. Nonetheless, it is easy to understand why and how most or all of these requirements are unrealizable and, thus, violated. And then, qualifying factors for applying tests of statistical significance and determining probability quotients themselves are routinely violated. For example, tests of statistical significance depend on precision of the criteria, that is, their reliability, and power for positive results, that is, the number of students who participate in an experiment. The more students, the more power and degrees of freedom, and thus the more assurance to declare a robust statistically significant difference has been established. But nonetheless, the difference may or may not in fact actually exist. This dilemma has been recognized by some contemporary music education researchers, thus motivating them to make a distinction between quantitative research, that is, what I have been describing, and qualitative research, that is, dismissing statistical analyses and as an alternative, embracing methodological triangulation and critical observation.

Mason Is engaging in any type of music education research a fruitless mission?

Orff No! May I offer a dictionary definition of the word "empirical?" "Relying on or derived from observation or experiment. Guided by practical experience or theory." In resistance to success laypersons have enjoyed historically, regardless of whether results relied directly or indirectly on knowledge derived from commonplace observation, descrying has been disregarded for centuries by many academics as unworthy of consideration and undeserving of respect. In my opinion, that is misguided. Allow me to explain why.

Consider a curious child who touches a hot stove as an example of quick and simple empiricism. Barring harm to the child, the procedure is elegant and unpretentious. Results are obvious and immediately generalized. With even a modicum of intelligence, the child will not make it a practice of touching a hot stove. And think of the proverbial cat that learns rapidly to see before being seen when another animal or human enters a room, or the lovable dog that enthusiastically offers tricks for food.

Kodály Continue, Carl.

Orff Whether driven by intuition with humans or instinct with animals, empirical inquiry engenders valid knowledge and understanding. Sagacious empirical researchers have theories that direct inquiry and make biases obvious. They replicate inquiries under a variety of conditions to determine if results are steadfast, and when they are not, researchers undertake new examinations to acquire more advanced or new information. Better yet, they encourage others to pursue similar experiences and empirical inquiry to cross-validate, that is, corroborate, results that may or may not be serendipitous.

Particularly in empirical inquiry, it is disagreement with one's own previous research results and disagreement with colleagues' conclusions that advances human cognition. After all, any intelligent person knows results of one piece of research do not constitute ultimate truth. Though it may sound uncanny, good research is so well designed and conducted that results it offers may be replicated or disproved.

Corybant Thank you all for explanations, perceptions, and proclivities.

XVII: Interlude

Corybant Surprise! Good news! You have inquired about the possibility of gathering again. In researching that likelihood, I discovered I misinterpreted some earlier computations and thus, it is apparent we have time for not just one, but two more sessions! I hope that pleases you and forgiveness will be granted for my temporary lacuna of mind.

I have given thought to what our new penultimate topic might be. Thus, I have a suggestion, prompted primarily by our last discussion about research. As you remember, we talked about the difference between objective and subjective research. Differences, however, go beyond what we have spoken. I'm referring to pedagogical research, which we have examined, compared with medical research. Specifically, there is research in the psychology of music and also in the neurology of music. Though research in the two disciplines reflects different intents, the results they reveal in some respects impinge on one another. They are not totally dichotomous. Despite some disparities, knowledge of neurological research pertaining to amusia should be of great interest to you. Obviously, most of the advanced work in neurological research has been undertaken since your lifetimes. Are you interested in this topic?

Wait, my question is premature. Because this neurological research has taken place in the recent past, you may wonder how you can carry on an intelligent conversation without having adequate information. I have taken care of that barrier.

My aide, the assistant chief, directed her chief assistants to prowl earth and collect relevant information about recent neurological research they think might be of interest to you. I made suggestions, of course, based on my reading. Aides were not to return with books but rather, to make copies of noteworthy pages from iconic books. That is illegal on earth, of course, but when authors and publishers arrive here, they see our economic system is radically different from what it is below.

Each one of you will receive a particular anthology that comprises special interrelated topics most closely allied with your interests. Of course, you need time for recumbent reading. Take the remainder of the cock-crow to peruse the documents. Shall we reconvene near midday?

XVIII: Neuroscience of Music

Corybant Welcome back, and a good afternoon to all.

Kodály To facilitate my reading, I requested an unabridged English dictionary to seek the definitions of two words. May I share them with you?

Corybant Please do.

Kodály "Amusia": A condition akin to aphasia resulting from brain lesion and marked by loss of ability to follow, understand, and appreciate music.
"Aphasia": A loss or impairment of power to use or understand speech, resulting from brain lesion, or sometimes, from functional or emotional disturbance.

Corybant Thank you Zoltán. I presume those two words will be pivotal in our dialogue. Now, how shall we begin?

Jaques-Dalcroze Well, here I am again. I read a litany of information about perfect pitch. I guess I am blessed, because I learned that approximately only one in 10,000 persons have the attribute. Not all of them become professional musicians, but those who do specialize and excel in conducting and composition. They report absolute pitch an asset. While not necessarily essential, it is extremely valuable. Mozart had it, but Wagner and Schumann, for example, did not.

Interestingly, 50% of children born blind or who become blind at an early age exhibit perfect pitch.

Corybant Yes, and a third of musical savants are blind or have poor vision. Although they demonstrate compleat musicality, they are weak in most other traits. And you know, there are also visual savants.

Jaques-Dalcroze Along with reports I received I came across some thoughts I found disturbing. In interview and questionnaire research, musicians with perfect pitch not only have trouble when playing a transposing music instrument, they also are uncomfortable when asked to transpose familiar music. Reading and performing in one key while simultaneously inner hearing the same music in another key is, to say the least, disconcerting.

It is said absolute pitch comes and goes. A person may possess it on one occasion but not on another, perhaps because of emotional or physical stress. Of course, surgery can have deleterious effects, loss of absolute pitch notwithstanding. And don't discount the power of accidents and lightning in that regard.

Kodály Émile, has your attitude toward attempting to teach perfect pitch changed?

Jaques-Dalcroze Based on reading, the benefits and hazards that accompany perfect pitch appear to be equally weighted, but I would not forfeit it under any circumstances. And by the way, I did not attempt to teach perfect pitch. I determined it was acquired naturally under favorable conditions.

Seashore My material included a snippet about perfect pitch. Thus, I must offer a caveat about the phrase "born with." As a scientist, I believe specificity is a mandate. It is reputed persons are born with potential to develop perfect pitch, which is a high level of tonal aptitude. The achievement of perfect pitch, however, is a result of cultural environment. It is learned. Again, we are confronted with

XVIII: Neuroscience of Music

the difference between aptitude and achievement, which is essential to specificity.

von Laban Of course, Carl, what you say makes sense. It is ludicrous to presume children are born with perfect pitch indigenous to their individual cultures in terms of a particular scale that incorporates half and whole steps, or quarter tones.

Seashore Yes, the chance of that occurring is no greater than we all are to become mortal once again in the next moment.

von Laban Carl, I agree, but is it possible a child in utero might acquire perfect pitch indicative of a given culture?

Seashore I doubt it, but who knows what astounding future neurological research will reveal? For now, research indicates if a pregnant woman presses a cello close to her belly as she plays a specific composition, the child will recognize the sound after birth. An unborn child may vaguely associate parts of a composition, but identify and name individual pitches? I think not.

von Laban Mortality! A serendipitous occurrence in the adventure of being.

Mason Not to be dour, but even we immortals need to be logical. I think we must discuss amusia before we entertain other topics.

Corybant I gather amusia can be receptive or interpretive.

Kodály I think it is safe to say frontotemporal dementia precipitates most, if not all, cases of amusia, which, in turn, may manifest hypermusia and musicophilia. Musicophilia, sans other abnormal symptoms, is an intense, even acute, craving to hear or perform music. Hypermusia, a sensory-limbic hyperconnection, is an unusual and ineffable sensitivity to musical sounds of all types accompanied by loss of command to cope with language and abstractions. Maurice Ravel suffered from hypermusia in later life. On the other hand, there are persons, such as Sigmund Freud, James Joyce, and Charles Darwin who had little proclivity for music.

Mason Did Robert Schumann have hypermusia?

Kodály It is difficult to diagnose in retrospect. Consensus is he had general psychosis, but that doesn't exclude hypermusia.

von Laban What a delightful donnybrook would be in the making if Mr. Schumann were included in one of our future meeting.

Corybant I will take that into consideration.

Seashore About other types of amusia. Four were described in my portfolio. Tinnitus is typically accompanied by loud or soft musical hallucinations. The same music is heard repetitiously beyond the patient's wishes. Such echoic imagery can become pathological. Dystimbria prevents one from discriminating among tone qualities, and the person is continuously annoyed by cacophony. Dystonia is more a physical than psychological problem, where the brain and mind are in conflict. For example, a performer's fingers curl up and refuse to coincide with the performer's audiation. There, too, is musicogenic disease, which is discernible by a person's fear of music, particularly certain music instruments or pieces of music.

von Laban In addition to negatively affecting one's ability in musical performance, listening and memory in temporal lobe epilepsy can also hasten impulsive mystical feelings.

Orff I am spellbound by what I also learned about the brain. Most current research debunks earlier findings pertaining to functions of the left and right cerebral hemispheres. One of the latest discoveries is that rhythm permeates both hemispheres, whereas melody is located solely in the right hemisphere. Also, amnesia is prevalent for most cognitive functions except that which engages music, with one exception. One can experience emotional amusia. What I found most surprising is the right hemisphere develops before the left early in life. Nonetheless, shifts in hemispheric dominance can be simultaneous with abnormality.

Seashore I might as well mention a few more facts. Structurally understanding music and emotionally appreciating it requires different brain mechanisms. It is no wonder creative and rational processes in music are different. What's more, in the wake of trauma, the brain can reshape itself so that activity formerly associated with damaged sections can be transferred to another with little or no deficit. It seems to follow eidetic and mnemonic powers may be released under exceptional conditions.

Kodály My anthology informed me the corpus callosum, which is the great commissure that connects the two hemispheres of the brain, is enlarged in professional musicians. Moreover, the brains of musicians show increased volumes of gray matter in motor, auditory, and visuospatial areas of the cortex and cerebellum. And, Émile, this should especially interest you. The planum temporale, which is part of the auditory cortex, reveals an asymmetric enlargement for musicians who maintain they have perfect pitch.

In this connection, I assume you know about synesthesia, specifically chromesthesia. It has been identified in one in 2,000 persons. These individuals systematically associate colors, tastes, and objects with pitches and keys.

Orff Alexander Scriabin professed chromesthesia.

Kodály Oddly, synesthesia works backward, too. Colors, tastes, and objects can activate the sound of a given pitch or key. By no means, however, is there agreement among individuals in terms of associations.

Corybant I have vibes of Marcel Proust's Remembrance of Things Past.

Mason I culled a charming statement from my readings. "Every disease is a musical problem, every cure is a musical solution." That spurred me to recall stutterers enunciate words clearly when singing, musicians' tics disappear when performing, and persons in a post-encephalitic stage have enormous trouble moving but nonetheless, are able to dance rather gracefully.

von Laban It would seem the author of what I am about to paraphrase doesn't know the word "audiation." Nevertheless, he or she is well aware of its significance. It was said when listening to or performing music intellectually, one is concurrently hearing, recalling what was heard, and predicting what is about to be heard. Stated another way, the past can be present without being remembered, and the future can be present without foreknowing.

Seashore Now that we're talking about audiation again, I have an interesting thought. The literature given to me is replete with discussions of carpal tunnel syndrome. This tendonitis literally prevents a musician from performing. I propose this disease is not physical. I'll wager it is psychological. Specifically, if a musician cannot audiate what is to be performed, the muscles rebel in confusion and exhibit their own form of frustration.

Changing the subject, however, Corybant's reference to Proust calls to mind the subject of imagery. In 1880, Francis Galton called attention to visual imagery, but ignored musical imagery. His overlooking the latter might have enticed me early in my professional career to study musical imagery. When I was as a young man, I had no idea the brain treats visual and musical imagery differently. Furthermore, I learned this morning musical imagery is biologically adaptive.

Orff I am intrigued with the notion of normal illusion. It is possible to inner hear a phantom pitch while listening to its true counterpart as it is being physically sounded. It seems musicians are able to hear what they want to hear for reasons they can readily explain—reasons like being forced to sit through an unbearable performance or conducting an inept ensemble are often reported as being sources of the necessity.

von Laban We have talked much about tonal elements of music, but the text I read talked about recent developments in research about rhythm.

Orff Tell us about them.

von Laban Rhythm has been shown to bind persons into a group. Perhaps that explains the appeal of current Occidental popular music. Also, I learned although tone deafness is well documented, rhythm deafness does not exist, or it is elusive. Evidently, even though being a recipient of a cochlear implant may destroy pitch discrimination, it has virtually no effect on a person's sense of rhythm.

Jaques-Dalcroze I conjecture that is a result of the human mind and body naturally responding to vibrations with or without sound being present. Persons using iPods are increasingly impairing their hearing but nonetheless, their response to rhythm remains intact and normal. I presume we all read about ipods this morning?

Seashore I discovered the phenomenon of subjective rhythm in the early twentieth century. When sitting on a train and listening to wheels pass from one set of rails to another, even nonprofessional musicians impose duple and triple meter on what they are hearing, or should I say feeling?

Jaques-Dalcroze The same is true with the ticking of a clock. Humans are wired for rhythm.

Corybant No one has mentioned the profession of music therapy. Michigan State University in East Lansing Michigan, first introduced a degree in the discipline. If what I read is accurate, I'm impressed with how it can alter children's behavior. It can even interdict problems of autistic children.

If we only had time, I would like to know how recent neurological research might have already influenced the group's thinking. For example, some may have new beliefs about preferences for timbre and range, or different attitudes toward music aptitude. If and when we assemble again in the distant future, research developments will receive priority listing.

After experiencing demands of this session, I doubt you will need soporific incentives. I will greet you a little earlier than usual on the morrow.

XIX:
Exire: Thanks and Farewell

Corybant Oh my! I see sad faces. No need to be glum! We knew from the onset our separation was inevitable. Now, perk up. I have a novel proposition for you.

   Pretend you are asked to bestow one or more final messages to humans before you leave their region. Your messages may be brief or extended, and you may offer as many as you desire. Though not necessary, it would be preferable if the messages had continuity, that is, from one person to another. What might you say? Take a moment and try to predict what any one of your colleagues might say. I can almost guarantee your guesses will be astray. Does the idea appeal to you?

Mason Bully pulpits?

Corybant I trust not!

Seashore Let's try it. It should spawn enormous implications.

Suzuki Not only for us, but also for those still enmeshed in earthly trials and tribulations.

Corybant I have two endorsers. Anyone else?

Jaques-Dalcroze Corybant, I think it's a splendid plan. But, I'm not sure I want to share my innermost personal thoughts with anyone. I'm inclined to shyness. I dance better than speak.

Seashore I empathize with Èmile.

Kodály I suspect most of us do.

Corybant None of us is infallible.

von Laban That's not really the point. What particularly bothers me is, I don't wish to inadvertently confuse or shock my devotees who may still be vitally engaged in furthering my philosophy.

Corybant Alright! Let's do it this way. When you speak, do not reveal who you are. Only I will identify myself. What a great guessing game of speculation for our friends. To be sure, I am not expecting emanations, nor am I hoping to galvanize unity. The more we celebrate diversity, the better.

Orff Yes, diversity among ourselves is motivating, but I don't think it is a good model for earthlings. They experience sufficient pedagogical disagreements among themselves already and contend enough with sufficient criticism from, and are shunned by, many outside their profession. They don't need any more turmoil inside their discipline.

Corybant You make a point, but I have abundant faith in music educators below to give serious thought to what will be said. There is tremendous respect for all in the group. Acknowledging the possibility of a downside to constructive criticism, though coupled with accolades, ultimately, professionals know you all are sincere and have made significant positive contributions to individual music educators and music education at large. Do not fret!

Shall we begin? I see heads nodding in the affirmative. Who will offer the first message?

—I would like to say a few words about the dichotomy between education and entertainment in music education. Music teacher's primary mission is to educate students about music. Of secondary importance is entertainment of our wards, themselves, and their parents. If you easily surrender faithful ethos to the malaise of an uninformed bureaucracy wallowing in a phlegmatic bath of repugnancy, you are allowing insecurity to compromise music education.

Leaders of a national music education association have endorsed and supported findings that report more than 80% of persons with postgraduate degrees and those who earn a substantial income, far above average, participated in school music in the United States of America. What they fail to report is that shamefully, only a small minority of students who were members of school music ensembles continue active participation after graduation from high school. Does evading the second finding in part subliminally suggest the primary reasons music should be a component of a school curriculum are for purposes other than learning to understand music? Carrying this to an extreme, soon it could be recommended music schools be closed and music classes and performance groups become part of a university business school course of study.

I do not deny school performances have value for students socially, but to have value educationally, music programs should be outgrowths of what was or is being learned in music classrooms and rehearsal halls. When students spend most of their time in preparation of staging holiday presentations without understanding intrinsic elements of music they are performing, generalization vanishes from one program to another, or for that matter from year-to-year, for possibilities of acquisition of unadulterated musicianship. That, I feel, is unconscionable. It is telltale of asking what students can do for a school rather than what a school should do for students. Might I suggest such practice be considered academic prostitution?

Lead or follow! Should music educators, or it would be more appropriate to say musicians who teach music in the schools, show the public the way or should they tag behind popular trends and opinion? They best lead at least 51% and follow no more than 49%. It is a delicate commission that must be confronted using educational and artistic compasses. Courage is required, and above all, an attempt to justify ample time for music instruction in schools by claiming it enhances learning in other disciplines is demeaning. Music is strong enough to shield its own existence. No one in a school other than a capable music educator is able to guide students in learning to audiate, or, if you prefer, inner hear. Remember, fashions change, but style is eternal.

Corybant Thank you. I know your words will be given serious consideration.

—Etymology of the word "etiology" is rooted in the Latin word *aitia*, which may be translated as "cause." Another Latin word, "curriculum," arises from *currere*. It means to run. To my mind, the two words are linked in the pedagogical philosophy of music education. I would like to explain how and why.

The arts, music notwithstanding, have not fared well for centuries in comprehensive schools. When there is a crisis and education, euphemistically speaking, suffers from a common cold, the arts contract pneumonia. Their existence in a curriculum, even as extracurricular activities, is perennially threatened. It came to my attention, even recently, students with low grade point averages are punished by not being permitted to participate in music activities or athletics. That students' self esteem and confidence was jeopardized by disenfranchising them from achieving at high levels in perhaps the only fortes they could was of no concern to rule-makers. As compensation, the unfortunates are offered opiates of spectator sports, batting averages and football yardages, media trash, and loathsome tabloid photos and print. How are they to know a physically healthy life is festooned with severe limitations without the mind sensitively participating in one way or another in the arts? Life is art and art is life.

All said, music educators and administrators must share blame for decisive shortcomings. Succinctly, a worthy sequential music curriculum is absent in most schools. I take no joy in telling you music education continually follows the path of ritual rather than doctrine. Granting it may be nigh on to impossible to design a country or state music curriculum, certainly development of a local music curriculum is possible. Of course, teachers may organize an anthology of songs with allied teaching suggestions amid snippets of music notation and theoretical terminology, but that hardly qualifies as a sequential music curriculum.

XIX: Exire: *Thanks and Farewell*

Imagine a family who moves from one city or state to another and the new language and arithmetic teachers have no idea what your or another parent's fourth grade child had previously been taught, nor possesses any factual expectation of whether the student's background would permit him or her to learn what is currently being taught in class. Now, accept the fact, without tendering excuses, that is the typical case in music. It is unconscionable. And I might add, it is expected students' records will include scores on academic standardized achievement and intelligence tests, or if not that, at least results on related teacher-made tests. Records and scores pertaining to music aptitude and music achievement are nowhere to be found.

I am not suggesting you seek a shaman to invoke a mantra, but I leave it to you, current music educators, to give consideration to what could prove to be monumental change and improvement. That is, creation of a sequential music curriculum for your school district that emphasizes learning rather than teaching. If that seems unworkable, it would be exemplary to create a viable course of study for at least your own school

Take earnest notice of the possibility sensible music has become an endangered art as a result of post modernism and fragmentation. Do not teach the way you were taught or the way your were taught to teach without substantial professional reflection and review. And above all, as sentinels, do not surrender gently to unbridled uninformed immutability. Ideally, if causes of factiousness cannot be prevented, they must be abolished, and if they cannot be abolished, their effects must be controlled.

Corybant Thank you. Such advice carries broad implications.

—I assume most intended readers of this document teach music in elementary and secondary schools. I wish, however, college, conservatory, and university music faculty would also avail themselves of our presentation. Nevertheless, I believe diffusing our thoughts may in some way influence change from reluctance into gathering knowledge by professors in higher education.

It appears music faculties who prepare teachers to teach music in lower schools are impervious to the salient fact prospective teachers are receiving an inadequate education. As a result, problems arise in elementary and secondary schools for which music teachers are not entirely to blame. There is a preponderance of scheduling and other administrative problems, but incipient causative factors other than those are even more deeply entrenched in higher education.

In a majority of cases, future music teachers receive no guidance in music curriculum development. Lack of undergraduate and graduate education notwithstanding, for reasons associated with time constraints and extra musical responsibilities among many other interrelated factors, working teachers are unable to develop music curriculums on the job. For mentors to state otherwise is wishful thinking and abdication of accountability. In the end, it is left to senior colleagues to organize summer certification seminars and assume the mission, and with all due respect, information, direction, and continuity provided in such a paucity of time leave much to be desired.

We have heard about lack of knowledge of curriculum development on the part of professors and music teachers alike, but I have more to add. Another component almost nonexistent in higher education, especially in undergraduate school, is teacher preparation in test development and interpretation of subjective as well as objective test results. As music teachers move into positions in schools, they have little alternative but to depend upon their personal evaluations for awarding grades. That is a result of lack of knowledgeable wherewithal to take advantage of benefits objective measurement techniques offer, benefits, that is, to both teachers and students. And, historically, neglect of that vital component in the emergence of quality education is rarely, if ever, ameliorated by teachers themselves.

Corybant Your passion tells me you are not finished.

—No, I am not. I have another topic in mind.

Many students are so paralyzed in terms of physical movement it seems improbable they can ever come to terms realistically with musical rhythm. Nonetheless, they are taught rhythm by using their eyes rather than their entire body and ears. Rhythm patterns and rhythm solfege play no role in their education. Instead, students are relegated to perennial counting and unsteady foot tapping in search of a beat. I implore you to recognize importance of movement to overall musicianship, not only to rhythm, as you create worthy curriculums.

I would like to speak much longer, but I know others must be given an opportunity. For me to assess insufficiency of time devoted to student teaching as well as difficulties associated with disagreements between supervising and critic teachers would be preaching to the choir. So, I leave that issue and other important ones to your musing. I entreat you to recognize pedagogical problems and realize importance of engaging in earnest endeavors to discover solutions. To that extent, you may transform music education from a mere profession into a proud and respectable discipline. Do not seek help from above. It will not be forthcoming.

Corybant Thank you for offering so much to think about.

—As I follow up on the previous message, I have only a few things to say.

Whether due to insecurities or hubris, typically there is a chimerical division in philosophies and purposes in higher education between applied and academic music faculties on the one hand and professional music education faculties on the other. The two groups are like two sides of the same mountain, never observing or communicating with each. That, indeed, is regrettable. Ultimately, prospective music teachers suffer most. A marked improvement might take place if applied music teachers, theorists, and historians were required to observe student teachers as they begin to practice their careers in lower schools. Perhaps, then, reality would settle into minds of professors, and substantial relevant course content might come into existence.

You may be wondering if I will give a specific example of what I have said, and so I shall. It may seem inconsequential, but trust me, it is of great significance. I'm sure some of you already have experienced what I am about to relate. I refer to lack of cooperation and understanding among music theorists and music educators. Consider an average student who enters college or university as a music major, but nonetheless is deficient in the ability to audiate. At best he or she can imitate, memorize, and regurgitate definitions of music symbols in music notation. Regardless, music theorists insist on using fixed "do" or movable "do" with a "do" based minor, usually ignoring modes altogether, at the same time music educators are teaching movable "do" with a "la" based minor. Students' confusion and sacrifice of musicianship is egregiously and disingenuously extended exponentially.

You ask how can this happen? I wish I knew so I could offer a resolution to this as well as related ills indigenous to the academy. You, as music educators, could organize yourselves into powerful enclaves that challenge the precipitated maelstrom, and demand change. Remember, the most important changes that have taken place in your world are a result of small, persistent minorities pursuing truth. Given current exigencies, I sense a review of responsibilities of insulated, incompetent, tenured professors is already forthcoming.

Corybant Thank you. I am pleased we had the foresight to limit the length of the previous meeting. I'm sure your departure remarks are longer than any of us anticipated. That is not to say they are not welcome. Next, please.

—I have a few words to express pertaining to instrumental music. We have been reminded a student learns two instruments: the audiation instrument and the actual music instrument. In terms of sequential music vocabulary development, the audiation instrument must be learned first. With that accomplished, students should be able to sing and move to what they are expected to read in music notation. Thinking of the difference between education and entertainment and also contrasting notational audiation with decoding of symbols should be the rule.

What I have articulated implies students should be capable of performing instrumentally by virtue of their audiation ability before they are exposed to and expected to read music notation. Understand, imitation is not to be eschewed. It serves as a necessary requisite for acquiring audiation skill. Further, with acquisition of audiation dexterity, it should prove easy to engage students in improvisation. In fact, I suggest you experiment with teaching improvisation before you

XIX: Exire: Thanks and Farewell

teach students to read music notation. You will discover convincing benefits of that procedure.

Finally, guide students in hearing and identifying chord changes in harmonic progressions, first by ensemble singing and then performing in parts. Obviously, the jewel in the crown is harmonic improvisation. Preferably, after reading skills are attained, compositional creativity naturally follows. With sequential education, reading may validly be regarded as a final consideration. If all holds true to form, students by this time, for most intents and purposes, will have taught themselves to read music notation.

In this connection, I see no real need for students to receive lessons in music theory even after they can audiate, and certainly not before. When did you learn to parse a sentence or when were you taught grammar? After you could listen to, speak, and carry on a conversation, and read, and write your native language. I doubt when you uttered your first word, "mama," you were told it is a noun. That most likely would have curtailed further development of your language skills. To the same extent, music theory taught prematurely inhibits musical development. Though most of you have not been taught grammar, or if you have, what you learned has summarily been forgotten, you engage appropriately in language tasks. The same may be said for music theory and music performance, listening to music notwithstanding.

Corybant Thank you. Please speak.

—All testimonials I've heard have great merit. Nonetheless, not intending to be untoward, I must remind all an important component has thus far has been neglected in this final gathering. It is early childhood music and movement. We all know teaching preschool music offers scant recognition relative to directing ensemble performances. But remember, Charles Ives said trophies, awards, and prizes are badges of mediocrity.

We have listened to caveats concerning what further deterioration may occur in the absence of sequential music curriculums in lower schools and perpetuation of inappropriate ones in higher education. However, only a few alert music educators over the years have called attention to the crucial role of early childhood music and movement education in curriculum development. Currently, many more classroom specialists talk about the necessity of providing language arts and arithmetic guidance to youngsters who are still in the home than there are music educators who insist on making music and movement education available to preschool children. We need more educators to oversee and rectify that oversight.

Music professors must not consider it beneath their dignity to become knowledgeable about relevant and suitable pedagogical procedures for children younger than age five. Who else is better qualified than musicians to assist parents in rearing their offspring? Because many parents themselves were musically deprived as youngsters, and maybe throughout their lives, they need surrogate professional help, if for no other reasons than they are fraught with fear of their own musical incompetence.

I don't need to remind you what results would be if children were not acculturated in language until they received formal education in school. It would be a national disaster. The same situation prevails for music and movement, but major professional organizations and educationalists allow that understanding to evade their perception, and offer virtually no responsible answerability. I predict unless music and movement education become staples for children beginning at birth, the intolerable situation in music education, and I emphasize the word "education" not "entertainment," cannot be set right anymore than it could only be patched up if children were similarly not acculturated in language before entering school.

I urge you, the community of professional music educators, to give the sequential nature of preparatory audiation solemn deliberation. It matters not whether you currently teach classroom music or instrumental music at either the elementary or secondary school level, or if you teach music privately. Place yourself in the mix, mingle on the floor with babies and young children, and guide them in absorbing the sound of music. I guarantee unequivocally whatever else you are teaching, your efforts will display marked benefits for children when they participate as students in future school activities.

An added advantage will be your own current level of musicianship will improve dramatically as a result of rediscovering your childhood,

XIX: Exire: Thanks and Farewell

perhaps even discovering the one stolen from you. Moreover, young children can generously teach you more than you ever learned in school. You may even learn more than the children. Know you are in a more enviable position than your predecessors. As a result of research, there are now books written specifically to guide musicians in gainfully spending time with babies and young children. Should you take my advice, always keep in mind there is a difference between informal guidance and formal instruction. Your thought processes are best focused on the former in direct proportion to the latter.

Corybant Thank you. Don't feel rushed.

—There is a brief topic most music educators are derelict in recognizing. Please don't interpret what I will say as being sourced in anger or cynicism. If anything, it might be skepticism.

As practicing music educators, keep your own counsel in improving music education. Be wary of educationalists and bureaucrats. They are usually not qualified music teachers themselves, but are always available to pontificate and offer rapacious advice to those who have more actual contemporary teaching experience than they. Some of them believe music education is nothing more than fielding a marching band. You may easily recognize the offenders as ambitious, jaded persons who have gained political power for themselves and thus, secured authoritative positions as minions who impose unrealistic conditions for teacher certification. Also, they are not shy about publishing mandates and theoretical goals as well as quixotic standards that look good on paper but are unrealistic for practical implementation. Unworkable suggestions of the past are appropriated, given new wrappings and names, and presented as current spawned innovations and improvements.

The fire of goals and standards sheds no light. It only fills unbounded space with smoke. Be cautious of contingent shards of putative respect for your efforts and profession. Honor and trust thine own intuition. Be wary of the false scraps of respect thrown your way.

Corybant I wish we had more time to think about what we have heard, However, others desire to speak for the first time, and others want to express more thoughts. Let's go on.

—Speaking of neglected topics, there is a problem with the dearth of research in music education currently being undertaken. I see causes as twofold. Teachers are rarely, if at all, instructed in research practices. Sadly, graduate music education courses have mostly been relegated to reviewing material introduced in undergraduate music education methods courses. It is not unlike throwing good money after bad.

The other cause may be more detrimental. A minority of music educators are capable of and keen on doing research, but conditions in schools prevent them from doing so. In the past that was not the case. But perhaps mainly due to current litigious fears and emphasis on competition in students' academic achievement among teachers, cooperation from school administrators and districts are no longer forthcoming. Other impediments in attenuation are parents' objections to instructional time being diverted to their children's participation in research. Extraneous curricular activities can interrupt research plans. Finally, a United States census reports indicates 75% of families move every five years. As a result, an unstable student population precludes possibilities for conducting longitudinal research. Unfortunately, I see no resolution to that impasse. Perhaps you and others might.

There is, however, a more persistent problem. As I have said, a few music teachers are eager to participate in research activities, but more than not they are prevented from doing so. The problem circles back to school officials wary of research undertaken in schools in which they are administrators. The main reason for this was precipitated by some unthinking psychologists in the past who engaged young children in research using questionable techniques. Thus, now, mounds of paperwork must be completed and individual parents must grant permission for any research to commence. Then members of school human resource committees also need to approve research plans. Unfortunately and typically, they are not well-versed in overall research techniques. Furthermore, they usually are not knowledgeable of the needs associated with specific academic subjects. These committees are reluctant to approve proposals and thus, research is virtually stalled. The Peter principle, again, rears its ugly head and takes its toll.

Corybant Yes. Thank you for being willing to enter the proceedings.

—In the 20th century, Orff and Kodály approaches became popular in countermanding stereotypical elementary classroom music instruction, particularly in the United States, that centered on music appreciation and strained singing, and later, fads referred to as aesthetic and multicultural education. All have faded or on the verge of fading. In many cases, teachers had no choice but to assume roles of metaphor merchants, traders in analogies, and symbol mongers. Also, it was not uncommon for songs they were expected to teach to include G above the treble staff. New ideas were a welcomed relief.

However, most positive innovations bring unforeseen results. One, for example, is research opportunities are diminished because students are rarely taught, and thus no longer share, a common repertoire of songs, folk songs notwithstanding. Without familiar songs to serve a practical role in designing and conducting investigations, educational research has been impaired, if not hindered or totally mired.

My overall point is this: without continual reexamination of content and techniques pertinent to teaching music, pedagogy will maintain a status quo. The need for and possibility of valid change is necessary to sustain professional endeavors. Therefore, I ask you to be willing to participate in research whenever feasible and assist researchers in any way you can. You owe that to yourselves, your students, and future teachers.

Corybant Thank you. It seems challenges remain the same, but solutions change.

—I am aware time is limited, so I will get directly to the point. When the following story was first brought to my attention, I was amused. Now I am alarmed. Recent research findings supposedly indicate if children listen to music, they will become more intelligent. Be clear! Music is by no means an exceptional activity. Any action children engage in will make them more intelligent.

Soon after the report appeared in mass media, single-minded music teachers and administrators claimed if students were members of school instrumental and vocal ensembles, they would definitely achieve at higher levels in academic subjects. The possibility did not enter their minds, or perhaps it did but was cleverly overlooked, that because students were already achieving at high levels and thus, did not require as much study time as others, they had opportunity to participate in music ensembles as well as extracurricular activities. Cause was being confused with relationship. Nonetheless, the myth continues to be told, and there are believers. And astonishing as it may be, sponsored government research was recently undertaken to prove listening to the music of Mozart will reduce one's deleterious reaction to latex. What next? I am concerned because if and when truth is revealed, it is possible the music education profession will receive partial, or even entire, blame for the befuddled propaganda. Do what you can to debunk gibberish and be cautious of those who in their hearts are naysayers.

Corybant Thank you. I am surprised and taken aback by what has been revealed. I see there are two more statement to be made.

—I, too, will be brief. Be cautious of becoming beguiled by modern technology for teaching music. Nothing can replace a proficient teacher. If you think students can learn to audiate by composing at a computer, you are either engaging in wishful thinking or confessing that you yourself are unsure of how to teach music essentials.

Also, I must ask, is it truly important to music education to discover that a specific part of the brain is the seat of music comprehension? I think not. Why is it embarked on? Professors keep themselves busy that way, and publishable endeavors contribute to promotion and tenure. Albeit, remember, singing and movement are of the essence.

Corybant And now the final few words.

—I hope I have not delayed my thoughts on the matter of content and context too long. It is the concept of context that pleads for elaboration, however, not content, the latter being emblematic of tonal and rhythm patterns. Unfortunately, I cannot be as brief as my predecessor.

There is primary and comprehensive context in music. The former, as explained, refers to tonality and meter. The latter, of course, incorporates primary context as it relates, for example, to musical style, expression, interpretation, and tone quality, and listeners' ability to audiate inner and lower parts of a composition. To appreciate form in music, all else is requisite.

When audiating complexity in context, a listener anticipates what is forthcoming in familiar music and predicts what will summarily be heard in unfamiliar music. Ultimate enjoyment comes in responding to music when what is predicted by members of an audience is circumvented by composers or performers. That is, an alternate and appropriate melody or harmonic structure, for example, is substituted for expectation.

Deviation from probability and what might be considered the norm excites understanding and enjoyment of music. Mozart in classical music, Frank Sinatra and Miles Davis in popular music and jazz, and Pablo Picasso in visual art are masters in using silence or space to achieve aesthetic quintessence. Persons who don't know what they don't know, and thus are relegated to listening to music superficially, are at a disadvantage. Though not as simple as it sounds, it is music educators' responsibility to contribute to the prevention or amelioration of persons' undeserved musical disabilities and to guide their way to truly gratifying enjoyment of music through understanding.

Corybant I judge none of us are expecting, or would like to proffer a synoptic summary. To my mind, one seems almost impossible. However, I would like to offer a few words. After listening to all that has been said, I am convinced there is consubstantiality among you. There are many paths to truth in pedagogical philosophy, but all share the same name. We may not know what that truth is, but we certainly know what it is not.

I have a heavy, hollow feeling knowing the closing stage of our time together is imminent, if not already upon us. There is time, however, for me to remind you of Robin's—Puck's—last lines from Shakespeare's A Midsummer Night's Dream.

> If we shadows have offended,
> Think but this (and all is mended)
> That you have but slumbered here,
> While these Visions did appear.
> And this weak and idle theme,
> No more yielding but a dream,
> Gentles, do no reprehend.
> If you pardon, we will mend.
> And as I am an honest Puck
> If we have unearned luck,
> Now to 'scape the Serpent's tongue,
> We will make amends e'er long:
> Else the Puck a liar call.
> So good night unto you all.
> Give me your hands, if we be friends,
> And Robin shall restore amends.

As your spirits slip silently into the ethereal mist my dear friends, stay well and take comfort in knowing your professional avatar contributions will forever be remembered and appreciated. Rabbis who wrote the Talmud would be pleased. You gave much more than you took.

Index

ability 14
absolute/perfect pitch . 39, 42, 43, 71-73, 175-179
abstractions 35
accents 34, 52, 103, 107, 111
aesthetics 44, 197
age 27
alphabet 38, 92
amusia 175, 177, 179
amnesia 178
anacrusis 54
anhemitonic 43, 44, 51, 94, 130, 136
anthologies 150
anticipation 63
aphasia 175
appreciation 38
approach 31, 33, 40, 42
arrhythmia 155
arithmetic 53
arts 20, 186
assessment 84, 85
assumptions/limitations . . 170, 171
atomistic theory 17
atonal 96, 100, 101
audiation 27, 46, 54, 55, 61-69, 118, 123, 124, 129, 135, 146, 149, 180, 190, 197
audiation/actual instruments 123, 190
audiometer 17
aural/oral 66
aural audiences 46
aural perception 62, 65
autism 66, 181

babble 65, 66
balance 34, 53, 55
ballet 56, 116
beams 34, 35
beat functions 45
beats 34, 104-107
blues 55
body percussion 52
books 34, 36, 37, 39, 46, 58, 61, 91, 100, 104, 109, 112, 128, 133, 142, 179
brain/body . . 56, 57, 64, 146, 178, 179, 196
breathing 54, 120, 142
buckwheat-notes 34

cadenzas 139
carpal tunnel syndrome 180
causation 19, 196
cerebellum 179
certification 193
chaining 154
chant 130, 158
character notation 34
characteristic pitches 96, 97
chords 141, 142, 191
chromatics 38, 97, 131
chromesthesia 179

chronograph. 17
clapping 34
classroom music 150, 164, 195
cochlear implant 181
colors 179
Communists. 5
comparisons 146
compensatory. 152, 160
computers. 56, 196
concepts 31
conservation. 131
consonance/dissonance 57
consonance/dissonance body
    movement. 57
contemporary music. 42
content/context 63, 66, 73,
    92, 93, 101, 128, 141,
    154, 196, 197
Continental system 37, 38
coordination. 51, 142
corpus callosum 179
correlation 19, 20, 75, 76
cortex. 179
Corybant 1, 2, 9
counterpoint 95
counting. 34, 41, 53, 56,
    103, 189
creativity 10, 22. 35, 36,
    52, 54, 66, 137, 148, 191
crusis. 54
culture 32, 36, 43
curriculum 32, 33, 82, 89,
    145-155, 185-187
Cybele 1, 2, 9, 22,
    71, 157, 158, 167

dance 4-6, 40-43, 49-59,
    75, 110, 115, 180
dance choir. 111
dashes. 41
decoding. 65, 124, 138, 190
deductive/inductive 168, 169
diachronic 145
diagnosis. 25, 88
difference/sameness 146
difficulty 122
difficulty levels . 129-132, 142, 143
disadvantaged/advantaged. 25
discovery/experience 52
discrimination 20, 22, 28
distance 54
divisions. 45
"do" based minor 38
"do" signature. 98, 99
dots. 41
dropouts 163, 164
durations 52, 57, 73, 128, 140
dynamics 52
dystimbria. 178
dystonia 178

ear training. . . . 35, 52, 71-74, 140
early childhood music/
    movement. . . . 31, 51, 151-153,
    191, 192
echoic imagery. 178
education 10, 33, 67,
    117, 184, 185, 190
eidetic/mnemonic 179
Elemental Music 6, 33
emotion 22, 23, 25, 103, 135

empiricism 63, 171, 172
energy. .53
enharmonic/enrhythmic .107, 108
ensembles. 112
entertainment 184, 185, 190
environment . . 14-16, 27, 75, 119
errors .136
ethnomusicology 5
Eurhythmics. 3, 6, 52,
53, 111, 115
evaluation 79, 80, 83
experimentation. 52, 63
exploration. 5, 53, 136
expression. 22, 24, 43,
52, 53, 121
extra musical factors 16

fashion/style. 186
first endings 139
fixed "do" 38-40
flags. 34
flow. 53-57
folk dancing 51
folk music. 3, 5, 6, 40, 43,
44, 49, 51, 94, 95, 127
form 52, 197
formal instruction 152, 193
framework 42
fractions 103
fragmentation. 187
free-flowing continuous
    movement. 53-56
frontotemporal demensia. .28, 177

generalization. 50, 63, 83, 47
genetics 14, 17, 39

Gestalt 17, 146
gifted/talented 76
goals/standards 193
grading 79-89, 188
gravity .53
great commissure 179
growth 84, 85
Guidonian hand. 99
gymnastics 6, 51

half steps. 130
hand signs. 44, 46, 47
harmonic patterns 139, 141
harmonic progressions . . 137, 139,
141, 191
hearing. 35
Hellerau .5
hemispheric dominance. 196
heredity 15, 21, 27
higher education 187, 188
hinged mosaic relationships. . .146
historiography 169
history 33, 34, 59
horizontal/vertical 74, 93, 141
hypermusical 177, 178

identification 72, 119
idiographic. 83, 84, 88
inference 50, 82, 147
inflection 131
inhibition. 15
intensity. 140
imagery. 15, 180
imitation 52, 61, 64-67,
123, 135, 148
immovable "do" 37, 39, 42

improvisation........ 34, 35, 52, 54, 66, 94, 111, 135-143, 148, 149, 190
individual pitches/durations ..131
individual musical differences . 25, 36, 71-76, 84, 119, 122, 129, 142
informal guidance 152, 193
innate................15, 21, 27
inner hearing....... 64, 72, 111, 118, 119
inside-outside................50
intelligence 16, 18
interpretation.............22, 24
intervals......40, 68, 72, 74, 101
intonation....... 47, 54, 72, 74, 120, 121
instruction..........35, 67, 117
instruments ...7, 52, 67, 115-125, 136, 159-165, 190, 191
intelligence 76

Jaques-Dalcroze, Émile.......3, 4
jazz......................55
jump.....................54

key signature 98, 99
keyality..................98, 99
keys....................96, 99
kinesthetic.................52
kinetography.............4, 56
Kodály, Zoltán............5, 6

"la" based minor.............38
Laban, Rudolf von..........4, 5
Labanotation 4

language....... 7, 40, 62, 63, 66, 67, 118, 120, 151-154, 191, 192
lead/follow 185
learning....... 50, 121, 145-155
lessons 76, 111, 122, 138
letter names 38
ligatures 45
lines 41
linguistics.................5, 64
listening...........35, 39, 120
literacy....................43

macrobeats...... 45, 55, 104-112
major 38, 51
march....................55
Mason, Lowell 2, 3
measure signatures 106
measurement 79, 80, 83, 188
media....................152
melodic patterns......... 94, 132, 137, 154
melody 51, 84
memorization.. 40, 50, 64, 67, 68, 82, 118, 121, 123, 135, 148
memory 67
metacrusis..................54
meter 34, 44, 54, 103-109
 intact/unusual/usual .. 104, 105, 110, 111
meter signatures........ 106-110
method....31, 32, 40-42, 50, 136, 147, 150, 194
microbeats...... 45, 55, 104-112
minor 38, 51, 130
minor third..................51

mnemonics 179
modal 96
mode 95, 96
model 42
modes 38, 39, 44, 73, 95, 96
movable "do" 37-39, 97
movement 4, 22, 34, 40-43,
     49-59, 103, 110, 115,
    120, 137, 140, 142, 192
Mozart effect 195, 196
multicultural 195
multikeyal 100
multi-level 85
multimetric 112
multitemporal 112
multitonal 100, 101
multiple patterns 154
muscles 54, 56
music achievement . . . 13, 14, 18,
      19, 20, 24, 25, 28, 75,
      79-89, 119, 176, 177
music aptitudes 4, 10, 13-29,
     61, 75, 77, 92-94, 119,
      159, 176, 177, 182
 developmental/stabilized. 26, 27,
         61, 65, 66
music education . . . 5, 6, 9, 10, 21,
     31-33, 39, 49, 57, 185-198
music therapy 181
music theory 34, 38, 39,
      91, 92, 99, 91, 92, 99,
     125, 136, 141, 148, 191
musical ear 68
musicogenic 178
musicophilia 177

nature/nurture 28
Nazis 5, 57-59
neurology 64, 173, 175-182
newborns 57
normal distribution 25
normal illusion 180
normative 83-85
norms 15-17, 27, 77, 81, 82
notation 7, 34, 36-39,
       53, 56, 65, 67
notational audiation . 65, 149, 190
nuance 22
null hypothesis 165
numbers 87, 97, 98

objectivity 18, 79, 85
observation 171
omnibus theory 17
ontogenetic 51, 145
opera 116
option responses 28
Orff, Carl 6
over learning 122

pantonality 100
parents 119, 122, 153, 164
part writing 141
participation 75
pedagogy 31-48, 51, 71-77,
       120, 121, 130
pentatonic 43, 51, 94, 96,
        130, 136
percentile ranks 27, 82, 86
perfect color 43
perfect tempo 73
performance 81, 86, 87, 185

Pestalozzi, Johann Heinrich . . 3, 5, 36, 40, 46, 52
philosophy 31, 34, 41, 42
phrasing 52, 55, 140
phylogenetic. 51, 145
physical characteristics . 123, 124, 157, 160
piano/organ 52, 112, 118, 162
pitches 47, 72, 73 92, 128, 133, 141
pitch selector 124
planum temporale 179
plastique animée 52
politics 193
post modernism 187
power/precision 171
practice. 18
pragmatism. 42
pretest/post test 84, 85
practical/philosophical. 168
practice/training. 18
practice before theory 36
prediction. 63, 159
preference, non-preference measure 23, 24
preparatory audiation. 61-69, 153, 192
preschool 31
principles 41, 42
probability 169
professors 153, 187, 188, 192
psychology 4, 13, 17, 24, 194
psychology of music . . . 4, 133, 173
public schools. 32, 33
pulse. 34

qualitative/quantitative 171
range preference. . . . 124, 157-165, 182
rating scales 81, 86, 87
raw scores. 27
readiness. 142, 143
reading . . . 7, 34-36, 39, 43-45, 56, 121, 124, 125, 135, 137, 138, 191
recognition. 24, 72
recordings. 120
relationship 146
relative pitch 72
reliability 19, 26, 81, 86, 161, 171
religion. 33, 58
remedial 152
re-membered 155
repertories 195
re-search. 194, 195
research 17, 63, 64, 67, 74, 129, 162, 167-173, 194-196
resting tone 38, 64, 68, 69, 74, 97, 118, 130, 154
retroactive inhibition. 97
riffs 135
rhythm 6, 34, 37, 40, 41, 49, 51-53, 103-113, 181, 188, 189
rhythm patterns . . 45, 55, 73, 104, 127-134, 154, 188, 197
rhythm solfege 41-46, 188
Roman "do" 37, 39
rote. 35, 64, 121
rubato. 52
rudiments 36

savants .176
scales 39, 44, 72, 74, 94, 130, 177
Schulwerk 51, 67
science .15
Seashore, Carl 4
sensitivity 43, 52
sensory-limbic
  hyperconnection. 177
sequence. 31, 57, 67, 87,
                        136, 148, 150
sex 56
shadow movements 58
shape-notes 34-37
showing 35
sight reading. 124
simple/compound. 106-108
sine wave 22
singing 34, 35, 43, 67, 115,
              120, 132, 136, 163
singing before reading 36
singing schools. 35
solfege. 34, 37-41, 111, 190
sonance 141
sound before sight 35, 36
sound wave. 158
space. 53-57, 110
speaking 62
speech. 17, 40, 51, 63, 137
speech rhymes 51
spiritual expression. 37, 42
staff. 34, 41
statistical significance . . 164, 165,
                                        171
statistical tests 170
steady beat 51
stems. .34

stick notation. 41-44
stuttering 180
styles. 121, 133
subjective/objective rhythm . .181
subjectivity. 18, 66, 79, 85, 158
subtest 16, 23
summarizing. 63
Suzuki, Shinichi. 6, 7
symbols. 118
synchronic 145
synesthesia 179
synthesized sound. 160, 161
synthesizer 161
system. 32, 40, 42

talented, gifted, musical. . . 13, 16,
                                    17, 22
tapping 54, 189
taste .179
teaching 19, 5 0, 53, 145-155,
                            163, 187, 188
technique 7, 50, 118, 121, 147
temperament 43
tempo 52-54, 103, 104, 112
tempo markings 57
temporal lobe epilepsy 178
tendonitis. 180
tension 56
tests 15-20, 23, 24, 63, 77, 81,
    83, 85, 120, 159, 161, 187, 188
theater 4, 5
thinking 67, 68
tics 180
timbre. 158, 159
timbre preference. . . 157-165, 182
time 53, 55, 57, 110

time signatures 106
time values 41, 45, 53, 57, 106, 107
tinnitus. 178
tonal center 92, 118, 128, 154
tonal patterns 55, 127-134, 154, 197
tonality. 91-101
tone deaf. 72, 181
tone quality 124, 158, 159
tonic. 38, 47, 74
tonoscope. 17
transposition 43
triangulation 171
trilling 121

validity 18-20, 24, 25, 63, 81, 86, 120, 161
verbalization. 35
vibrato 121
violin 116, 117, 162
visuospatial. 179
vocabularies .67, 68, 137, 148, 154

wars .5, 59
weight. 53-57
what, why, when, how . . .149, 150
words 51, 92
writing 35, 43

About the Author

After receiving bachelors and masters degrees in string bass performance from the Eastman School of Music and a second masters degree in education from Ohio University, Dr. Gordon attended the University of Iowa, where he earned a PhD As a professor of music, he held the Carl E. Seashore Chair for Research in Music Education at Temple University, Philadelphia, where he was presented with both the Lindback and Great Teacher Awards. Prior to his association with Temple, Dr. Gordon taught at the University of Iowa and the State University of New York at Buffalo. At the University of Iowa, Dr. Gordon became General Editor of Studies in the Psychology of Music, and the school recently honored him with their Distinguished Alumni Award. Dr. Gordon was most recently inducted into the MENC Hall of Fame, and he is currently a research professor at the University of South Carolina.

Dr. Gordon's five most well-known books are *The Psychology of Music Teaching, Learning Sequences in Music, Introduction to Research and the Psychology of Music, Rhythm: Contrasting the Implications of Audiation and Notation*, and *A Music Learning Theory for Newborn and Young Children*. He has also written more than a dozen monographs and is a co-author of the general music series *Jump Right In: The Music Curriculum* and *Jump Right In: The Instrumental Series*. Included among the seven standardized tests he developed are the *Musical Aptitude Profile*; the *Primary, Intermediate, and Advanced Measure of Music Audiation*; the *Iowa Tests of Music Literacy*; the *Instrument Timbre Preference Test*; and the *Harmonic and Rhythm Improvisation Readiness Records*.

Dr. Gordon's primary interests are research in the psychology of music, music aptitudes, music-learning theory, and audiation. He presents seminars and lectures throughout the world, most recently in Germany, Belgium, Korea, China, Poland, Hungary, Portugal, Spain, Italy, Slovakia, England, Canada, Japan, and Hawaii. He also publishes widely in international research and professional journals.